MUSIC
OF OUR
TIMES

Eight Canadian Singer-Songwriters

Marco Adria

James Lorimer & Company Publishers
Toronto , 1990

A version of "Making Contact with Bruce Cockburn" appeared in *Canadian Forum*, November 1987.

Canadian Cataloguing in Publication Data

Adria, Marco L., 1959 -

Music of our times

Includes bibliographical references.
ISBN 1-55028-317-0 (bound) ISBN 1-55028-315-4 (pbk.)

1. Singers - Canada - Biography. 2. Composers - Canada - Biography.
3. Popular music - Canada - History and criticism. I. Title.

ML400.A37 1990   782.42'163'0922   C90-094005-0

Photo credits: **Gordon Lightfoot**–Early Morning Productions; **Leonard Cohen**–Dominique Isserman; **Neil Young**–Ebet Roberts; **Joni Mitchell**–Larry Klein; **Bruce Cockburn**–Finkelstein Management/True North; **Murray McLauchlan**–Roadside Attractions; **Jane Siberry**–Mark Abrahams; **k.d. lang**–Victoria Pearson.

James Lorimer & Company, Publishers
Egerton Ryerson Memorial Building
35 Britain Street
Toronto, Ontario M5A 1R7

Printed and bound in Canada

5 4 3 2 1 90 91 92 93 94

Contents

Contents

Introduction

Popular music has become a part of most social rituals in Canada, as it has in all of North America and, to a lesser extent, the rest of the world. Whether the occasion is a wedding or a curling bonspiel, whether the *shtick* is to sell gasoline or political candidates — popular music is usually considered appropriate. Thus, when I began thinking about writing a book on Canadian singer-songwriters, I knew the subject would have wide appeal.

But I discovered I was really on to something when I heard that Liberal house leader Herb Gray — yes, the man who talks a bit like Foghorn Leghorn — *adores* popular music. The *Edmonton Journal* reported in 1988 that Gray relaxes after Question Period by listening to the Rolling Stones or John Cougar Mellencamp. "At home," the item said, "he watches Much Music [the rock video channel] on TV. His kids are constantly after him to borrow his rock tapes." If this is not evidence that the river of popular culture (and in particular, its most powerful tributary, popular music) has flooded its banks and saturated Canadian society, I don't know what is.

Noel Coppage, an American popular music critic, has written that there is a *literati* in popular music, a group of composers whose music is characterized by reflection, refinement and taste. All eight of the singer-songwriters discussed here belong to this group; in fact they account for a large proportion of it. Gordon Lightfoot and Leonard Cohen, of course, carry with them the mystique of sustained, enormous success and the accomplishment of charting a career of almost twenty-five years. Both Neil Young and Joni Mitchell were at one time symbols of their generation, having written the counterculture anthems of the 1960s (Young's "Ohio" and Mitchell's "Woodstock"); more recently, they have been honoured not only by the popular music industry but by those critics of "serious" music who are also open to the wider possibilities of music. Similarly, Bruce Cockburn and Murray McLauchlan have gained the respect of their peers throughout the world for their artistic integrity. And as prominent members of the rising generation of musicians unafraid to challenge the bounds and definitions of popular music, Jane Siberry and k.d. lang have each established a unique place on the map of popular music. Simply put, this book is about some of the best popular musicians not only in Canada but also the world.

This is not a comprehensive history of Canadian popular music but a consideration of the life and work of some of Canada's popular soloists. All eight of these musicians were born or raised in Canada; they all write and perform their own songs; all have achieved substantial success through a combination of critical acclaim, performances, and a body of widely available recordings; all show the promise of remaining artistically active for some time. I have not tried to deal with French Canada's many singer-songwriters, since for the most part they have pursued their careers within the francophone community in Quebec and as such, the rest of the country has had limited access to their performances and recordings.

I have arranged the chapters chronologically, according to the release date of the subject's first album. Each essay is largely self-contained — that is, I have not tried to consider themes common to all the artists. Rather, I have considered each musician's career separately, addressing some of the social conditions that gave rise to it, the musical and lyrical aspects of the work, and how each musician has reacted to commercial success.

Still, some themes emerge. For example, Canadian singer-songwriters write and sing about frontiers. Consider such disparate examples as Gordon Lightfoot's song "Whispers of the North" and the wheat field pictured on the cover of k.d. lang's album *Absolute Torch and Twang*. If, as Robertson Davies has suggested, Canadians generally escape to the wilderness in order to forget who they are, these musicians are an exception, finding in their contemplations of nature a means to self-knowledge. As might be expected, the musicians' personal pursuits in this regard eventually find their way into the music. For example, Leonard Cohen's passion for cowboy mu-sic and Murray McLauchlan's hobby of flying in the northern bush have found expression in songs written by the two men. Even when the lyrics are really concerned with emotional or artistic frontiers rather than geographical ones, the expanses of northern and western Canada are often used as metaphors for freedom and individuality. As well, magical or spiritual forces are often treated in the lyrics. Bruce Cockburn has written about human love as a metaphor for divine love; Joni Mitchell has suggested that her collaboration with Charles Mingus was, if not pre-ordained, then at least blessed by happy coincidence. Although the mystical and the metaphysical are certainly not the prime concern of the respective bodies of work discussed here, it is difficult to ignore them.

The most striking similarity among the musicians is personal and professional, as well as artistic. All eight of them hold a curious dual conviction that they must reach for artistic heights — as defined by "serious" musical standards — while maintaining a mass audience. While all the musicians here have their roots in the "people's" musical idioms of folk, country and blues, every one of them also aspires to artistic accomplishment in the "musicianly" sense. The strength of the links between any one musician and either of these musical poles varies, of course. But I suspect that the tension that is created by such a stance — especially in light of the recent explosion of technology in the popular music industry, which can reduce a musician to functioning simply as a cog in the productional machine — constitutes much of the appeal of these musicians for their respective audiences.

A word on a couple of terms. First, *album* is as good a term as any to refer to what a record company releases as a recording. I use *album* as a generic term to refer to something that may have been released only in disc form or, more recently, one that is widely available only on compact disc or cassette. Second, I use the term *popular music* to refer to a broad category of music that is artistically accessible and widely available. The category includes folk, country, rock and blues. (Pop, on the other hand, is that narrower category of slick, "adult" music that still finds very wide appeal but that functions as a kind of emotional tranquilizer for its listeners; some call it "easy listening.")

I have included a "best" section for each chapter so that if you haven't heard anything of a particular musician — or heard very little — and you want to buy a recording, you'll have a starting point. My choices have been made according to numerous criteria that are admittedly and unashamedly subjective. Still, most of the "best albums" are widely available in commercial outlets; most of the "best articles" may be found in large public or university libraries.

I am grateful to Gordon Lightfoot, Bruce Cockburn, Murray McLauchlan and Jane Siberry for talking to me. And to Joni Mitchell for providing a bit of advice. Martin Arnold, Peter Chiaramonte and Richard Titus, all friends of mine, have heard some of the ideas here first. They, along with Bart Testa and David Gregory, provided helpful comments. Thanks to Curtis Fahey, Virginia Smith and Margaret Doane, accomplished editors at Lorimer, and to James Lorimer himself, who took a risk. The research and writing for this book was supported by funds provided by the Association for Canadian Studies made available by the Canadian Studies Directorate of the Department of the Secretary of State.

MA
Athabasca, Alberta
March 5, 1990

1·The Myth of Gordon Lightfoot

It's a gift from above
when we talk about love and romance.

— *"Romance"*

As you approach Orillia, Ontario, on Highway 12, there is a sign at the city limits that lists, as such signs always do, the appropriate civic messages, in descending order of importance:

City of Orillia
Population 24,000
Home of Gordon Lightfoot
"Support Your Hospital Fund"

It is not really Lightfoot's home, but his hometown, his birthplace. He doesn't live there anymore. But his likeness appears in the Hall of Fame at City Hall. And, according to the lady at the tourist booth, his mother, Jessie, still lives there.

Aside from the cluster of imposing and stately churches in the city core, Orillia is gloomy and even, in parts, grubby. Nothing is open on Sundays. Tourist season ends on Labour Day. Many of the public and private buildings in Orillia are built of brick: old brick, new brick, 1960s white brick, rusty brick, decaying brick, renovated brick. This is a city, one might say, of red-brick values — for brick is sensible, enduring, tasteful. Brick structures are put together block by block, with care and craft and workmanship. Just like a Lightfoot song. Only occasionally, Lightfoot uses his skills to fashion songs that some find overly commercial, too pretty. But that doesn't detract from the essential strength and structure of his work. He has chosen to make all things well.

Gordon Lightfoot has written songs about the expanses of Canada, about its history and legend. "Canadian Railroad Trilogy," for example, remains the most evocative — if not the most comprehensive — of the popular accounts of the building of the national railway. Parallel to Lightfoot's creative career, however, has been the careful refinement of a public persona. Lightfoot's stature as a popular musician — a result of the international recognition, the wealth — has set him apart from his song-writing colleagues in Canada. He has allowed himself to become a character in his own narrative. He has become both mythmaker and myth.

Gordon Meredith Lightfoot was born on Nov. 17, 1938. His musical training as a child was not extensive, but it engendered in him an attitude of seriousness towards music. He was encouraged to develop his musical skills by his parents, even though they were not particularly musical themselves. Lightfoot started singing when he was five years old. He sang solo in St. Paul's United Church in Orillia when he was ten or eleven. He also had piano lessons. Lightfoot's first recording ("Irish Lullaby"), made when he was only in grade four, was broadcast over the PA for a parent's day event. He sang in a barbershop quartet in high school and took up the guitar at sixteen. He also played in a couple of jazz bands. At one point he wanted to be a drummer. His interest in jazz carried over into some compositions he wrote for piano. He attended Westlake College of Music in Los Angeles in 1958, where he studied music theory, composition and arranging.

Lightfoot's early musical experiences, then, were diverse: vocal ensembles, jazz instrumental and folk. Lightfoot began singing in Toronto clubs with one of his fellow singers in the quartet, Terry Whalen. He then sang background vocals and danced on the CBC television show *Country Hoedown*, the forerunner of the *Tommy Hunter Show*. As a result of listening to the Weavers — an American folk group that was popular in the 1940s and 1950s and that included Pete Seeger as one of its members — Lightfoot's determination to pursue folk music was finally galvanized. His first recording, entitled *Lightfoot*, was released in 1965.

During his career, Lightfoot has won sixteen Juno Awards and the Juno "Hall of Fame" Award. He has three platinum records (signifying sales of 100,000 albums) and five gold (50,000) albums. A resident of Canada for virtually all of his life, he received the Order of Canada in 1970. He has four children: Fred and Ingrid, with Brita Olaisson (from whom he was divorced in 1973, after a ten-year marriage); Eric, with Cathy Coonley; and a baby boy, Miles, born in 1989, with his second wife, Elizabeth.

A Folksinger Is Born

Lightfoot has much in common with that group of North American singer-songwriters who forged the folk revival on this continent. The beginning of Lightfoot's career coincided with the tail-end of the folk revival, so Lightfoot is the youngest of the group. As a movement that was committed to preserving the legend and lore of the common people (actually, the common people of the US), the folk revival provided just the atmosphere for Lightfoot, as he was a musician who would later help to create and sustain the mythology of his own country. The singer-songwriter's important role in the folk revival would also figure in Lightfoot's personal and professional development, because Lightfoot was to become a popular, although solitary, figure of enormous success in Canada and internationally. The folk revival was marked by the rise of soloists; and even when some of his colleagues had joined ensembles of one kind or another, Lightfoot always composed and performed as a soloist.

The folk revival movement's beginnings can be traced to the efforts of John Lomax, an English professor from Texas A & M College who, in the first decade of this century, travelled through the American southwest with his Ediphone recording machine in tow, to save for posterity the cowboy songs and folk music of the old west. His collection provided the foundation for urban singers — such as Pete Seeger and Burl Ives — who brought folk music to a larger audience in the 1930s, 1940s and 1950s. Along with Woody Guthrie, who wrote "This Land Is Your Land" and "Roll on Columbia" — and, later, Tom Rush and Phil Ochs — Seeger and Ives were to influence a whole generation of folk musicians in the 1960s, perhaps most importantly Bob Dylan. That generation also included

Ian and Sylvia Tyson and Gordon Lightfoot. In his early days, Lightfoot included in his sets both his own compositions and those by Bob Dylan, Woody Guthrie and others. But it was Lightfoot's original songs that attracted the attention of his early audiences.

His first album showed the strong influence of the folk revival. The lyrics speak of the glories of forest and river and of innocent and mysterious love. Aside from Lightfoot's own compositions, the album includes "Changes," by Phil Ochs, and a prototypical folk revival song about the end of the world, "Pride of Man," by Hamilton Camp. As well, there is Lightfoot's own "Rich Man's Spiritual," a kind of parable in folk song form. The album is haunting, beautiful. Lightfoot's voice has never been sweeter.

One of the hits from the first album is "Early Morning Rain." While acknowledging the sensibilities of the folk revival, it also looks ahead to the confessional folk songs that would become the standard for so many singer-songwriters of the late 1960s. The lyrics make reference to freight trains and suggest that a jet the singer watches is an awesome living being, much in the way trains had been described in the folk revival. Lightfoot revises the myth of the iron horse: "Hear the mighty engines roar/ See the silver bird on high." There is also the idiomatic folk language: the cold wind, for example, "a-blows." Unlike a typical folk revival song, however, "Early Morning Rain" has an immediacy and sense of personal testament: the singer is cold and drunk. Even before Lightfoot recorded it, the song was covered by Ian and Sylvia Tyson; it thus provided one of the important stepping stones for Lightfoot's career. The Tysons' manager, Albert Grossman, signed Lightfoot to a recording contract, which resulted in the first album. Grossman was Bob Dylan's manager as well.

Like many other popular composers who started writing in the 1960s and 1970s, Lightfoot names Bob Dylan as his most important influence. Both musicians adopted a persona charged with mystery that was suited to their enormous popular stature and to their concern with writing and singing about myth. Lightfoot's relationship with Dylan goes back to the early 1960s, when Lightfoot began listening to Dylan's songs. As he told *Billboard*, the two met as a result of their mutual acquaintances, the Tysons: "I met Bob in Toronto at a party at

Ian and Sylvia Tyson's house early in his career. I've met him
several times since in various places around the country. When
I first heard Bob, I didn't want to copy what he was doing but
I realized he was moving into musical areas where angels fear
to tread, so to speak.... Lyrically and musically, he had an
extremely rural approach, which was partly in keeping with
my influences." Their friendship has endured. When Bob
Dylan's Rolling Thunder Review tour came through Toronto
in 1975, the entire troupe came to Lightfoot's home for a party.
When Lightfoot was inducted into the Juno Hall of Fame in
1986, Dylan presented the honour.

Yet although Dylan showed Lightfoot what a singer-songwriter could *be*, he did not influence what Lightfoot *did*. In fact,
it is Dylan, not Lightfoot, who has voiced "composer's envy,"
once expressing regret that he himself did not write "For
Lovin' Me." For Lightfoot's most important *musical* influence,
we must look, as I will discuss later, to the American south.

While many singer-songwriters of the folk revival, including Bob Dylan, tried to use their songs as a means to political
change, Lightfoot's only overtly political song has been the
song "Black Day in July," which deals with the riots in Detroit
of the late 1960s. Lightfoot's concern with artistic taste and
restraint has caused him to avoid veering in a direction that
his audience might consider extreme. However, in 1977, before
benefits for "causes" — as opposed to simply singing or talking about the world's problems — became common in the
world of popular music, Lightfoot donated the proceeds from
a concert at Avery Fisher Hall in New York to a campaign for
cerebral palsy research. He has been involved with many
charitable projects throughout his career. For example, his
voice is the first one to be heard on the Northern Lights for
Africa benefit single "Tears Are Not Enough."

Lightfoot and the Pop Idiom

Surprisingly, none of Lightfoot's first five albums, released by
United Artists, achieved spectacular sales. Still, they remain
enduring collections of fresh and compelling songs. In 1970,
Lightfoot moved from United Artists to Reprise. His first release with Reprise, *Sit Down Young Stranger*, recorded with
producer Lenny Waronker, was one of the most artistically
and commercially successful of his albums. (After "If You

Could Read My Mind" surfaced as a regional hit in Seattle, Reprise withdrew the albums and re-released them with the new title *If You Could Read My Mind.*) On the album, Lightfoot's sound became more "sophisticated" through the use of string arrangements and slick mixes. It sounded much more like a pop album than had his previous releases. (While "popular music" may refer to any music other than that of the academy, "pop" denotes accessible and attractive music intended for a large audience and is characterized by slick arrangements. Anne Murray is the prototypical "pop" performer, not just for Canada but for the whole world.) None of this detracted from the integrity of the songs, but here the problem of categorizing first arose.

The way an album is "positioned," to use the appropriate marketing term, has a significant effect on who will buy the album, since it determines where the album will end up, physically, on store shelves, which radio stations will consider playing a cut or two, and which advertising media will be chosen for promotion. And the positioning is determined by the "sound" of the album. *Sit Down Young Stranger* sounded like a pop album, even if so much of its mood was folk. Partly as a result of this, the album sold well in Canada and internationally. The single sold one million copies, which began the steady flow of wealth that in the best years has pushed Lightfoot's earnings to $7 million a year in royalties alone. (In the early 1980s, he was, according to *Toronto Life* magazine, still earning $1 million a year in royalties.) Lightfoot's relationship with Reprise continued until the first Warner Brothers release in 1978, *Endless Wire*. He is still with Warner Brothers today.

As a result of contractual obligations entered into in the 1960s, United Artists has released several Lightfoot compilations, sometimes in spite of Lightfoot's objections. These have included *The Best of Gordon Lightfoot*, *Classic Lightfoot*, *The Very Best of Gordon Lightfoot* (Volumes I and II) and *A Lightfoot Collection*. While Lightfoot receives royalties for the sales of these albums, their popularity can only eat away at the sales of his earliest, and even his more recent, releases. As a result, it is now very difficult to find anything in commercial outlets other than Lightfoot's most recent album and a couple of compilations. Lightfoot's own "official" compilations (*Gord's Gold* and *Gord's Gold Volume II)* are actually collections of re-recordings of his old hits along with the newer hits.

The Romantic Workman

While Lightfoot has released albums consistently over the years, 1972 saw a period of particularly intense creativity and productivity, with the release of two albums. Ironically, it was also the year he was diagnosed as having Bell's palsy, a degenerative nerve disease affecting the facial muscles, a condition from which he recovered but which has affected the use of his mouth and left eye. This is not the only debilitating condition that has affected him. Lightfoot has stated that drinking has been a detriment to his writing and to his career. In an interview published in *Canadian Composer* in 1986 — shortly after the release of *East of Midnight* — Lightfoot told interviewer Murray McLauchlan that he had taken his last drink in 1982 and intended never to drink again. Throughout these times, however, Lightfoot has never allowed his personal afflictions to affect his work. He considers his song-writing and performing to be a profession which he must protect from interference.

In this sense, Lightfoot's approach to writing has always been workmanlike. He has told the story of his voice teacher — who taught Lightfoot when the boy was only eleven years old — and the intensive practice Lightfoot undertook in order to compete in the local Kiwanis music festival, a cultural fixture of most small Canadian towns. He usually won the competitions. Thus was set a pattern of hard work and practice, followed by success, that he has maintained throughout his career. He often refers to the song-writing process as simply a matter of getting down to work. One of the qualities he says he strives for in a song is longevity, staying power. One is reminded of an artisan working in wood or, perhaps, leather — proud of his accomplishments, careful with his tools and reticent on the subject of his technique.

Significantly, he works with paper and pen, writing out the melody and lyrics, something that many other popular composers cannot or will not do. In an article in *Canadian Composer*, he was quoted as saying that his artistic goal is to continually improve, and that improvement comes from perseverance: "I try to be part of everyday goings' on; I don't think about the stratospheric aspect of things. I'm a working stiff, and I like to work and write, and I spend a lot of time on it and a lot of my personal life has gone down the tubes because of it. But I like my work, and I have no regrets." Lightfoot's workmanlike attitude has influenced his choice of session men, a small, loyal circle over the years. Red Shea and Terry Clements on electric guitar, Rick Haynes on bass, Pee Wee Charles on steel guitar, and Barry Keane on drums are the core of the group. Occasionally, Clements and Haynes accompanied Lightfoot on tour in the 1970s.

In spite of his wealth and privilege, then, Lightfoot has, in a way, *earned* a place in the working class, whose concerns are the subject of so many of his early lyrics. In so doing he has enlivened the legend of the noble worker, the myth of the Canadian working class.

Lightfoot's commitment to the craft of song-writing is confirmed by his dedication of "Your Love's Return" on *Sit Down Young Stranger* to the nineteenth-century American master songwriter Stephen Foster, who wrote such classic folk songs as "Old Folks at Home [Swanee River]" and "Beautiful Dreamer." The two songwriters' respective bodies of work reveal a common passion for taste, craftsmanship and the animation in song of legend and folklore. But citing Foster is something many of Lightfoot's contemporaries would not be likely to do. A search for the sources of popular music's tradition usually leads to the blues and to a celebration of black roots. (For Lightfoot, the title cut of *Sundown*, with its slightly flat electric guitar licks, is the only song to suggest anything of a blues influence. He acknowledges that his background was in the church choir, high school productions, operetta: "I didn't grow up in a place where the blues were heard all that much.")

In acknowledging Foster's influence on his writing, Lightfoot seems to trace his musical roots to the privileged society of the American south, the cradle of romanticism and chivalry in North America. For when Stephen Foster wrote about black life, in songs such as "Old Folks at Home," he was adopting a persona: while, in John Tasker Howard's words, Foster "assimilated the native influences with which he was surrounded," he was always, in fact, a member of the privileged class. For that matter, the North American folk revival, which influenced Lightfoot, was a movement largely involving white musicians and audiences. For his part, when I asked Lightfoot what his songs had in common with those of Foster, he named the simplicity and individual character of each melody. And he hinted at the formative importance of what a child learns to recite and sing: "We all took Stephen Foster songs in school," he said, "and some of that rubbed off on me. I was always a fan of Stephen Foster."

Lightfoot's own lyrics contain allusions to Foster's songs: consider Lightfoot's "banjo in my hands" ("Biscuit City") and Foster's famous "banjo on my knee" ("Oh! Susanna"), or Lightfoot's "I wonder how the old folks are tonight" ("Carefree Highway") and Foster's "That's where the old folks stay" ("Old Folks at Home").

There are other connections between Lightfoot's songs and Foster's songs. First, Foster wrote for the commercial market, without abandoning his innate artistic standards, just as Lightfoot has done. John Howard's reference to Foster in this regard applies equally to Lightfoot: "[The] market never soiled his work — it merely gave him a voice that could be understood." Second, for Lightfoot and for Foster alike, the autobiographical component is present in the songs, although most autobiographical detail is transformed or disguised by the exigencies of the "well-made" song. Third, both Lightfoot and Foster share a poetic stance of romanticism. In Foster's songs, this is made clear in the expressions of longing ("Old Folks at Home") and sensual imagery ("Jeanie with the Light Brown Hair"). In Lightfoot's work, romanticism is most evident in the contemplations of the Canadian wilderness, although the wilderness Lightfoot celebrates is not one that remains untouched by civilization. For him, the romanticism of the wilderness is complete only when man has imparted order to it, as the famous line from "Canadian Railroad Trilogy" states: "The green dark forest was too silent to be real." Thus, it is not the Canadian prairies and Rockies that he praises, but prairies and Rockies transformed by a pair of steel rails. It is not the land that is noble, but the land sown with the sweat and tears of the anonymous navvies. We can also see the romanticism in the imaginative names for women he has created in his songs: "Lavender," "Cotton Jenny," "Bitter Green," "Sundown," "Dream Street Rose" and "Knotty Pine."

Setting the Standards for Pop's *Literati*

Critic Noel Coppage states that, in his artistic approach, Light-foot is fundamentally different from his musical colleagues: "There is a *literati* in popular music, a group of people with refined musical taste, education and judgment, and my contention that Gordon Lightfoot is at the head of it just keeps getting more plausible with every record he makes." A *literati* implies an emphasis on technique and form, the common ground of artist and artisan. Three observations can be made about Lightfoot's adoption of the role of songwriter. First, song-writing is for him a craft that one works at with diligence. There is no substitute for attention to the tools of the trade, to careful work and pride of accomplishment. Second, the goal is to create something of beauty. This is not an assumption universally held by popular musicians. For some, the goal is to create something that "expresses" the writer's feelings most faithfully. For others — rockers, in particular — the goal is to provide a vehicle for affirmation of the self. For Lightfoot, the goal is aesthetic, not personal. Third, the criteria for beautiful things are not really to be questioned: they are to be found in the traditionally accepted standards of pleasing musical form and verse. In short, they are the standards of classicism. The classical aesthetic is characterized by formal balance, an emphasis on structure, and references to tradition.

Lightfoot's most enduring song, "If You Could Read My Mind," is, musically and lyrically, one of the most balanced of his compositions. The opening guitar figure continually returns to home. The opening lines of the lyrics answer one another. First, there is the statement: "If you could read my mind, love." Then the response: "What a tale my thoughts could tell." In the second verse, the lyrics are almost a restatement of the first, except that now the subject is the singer's lover: "If I could read your mind, love/ What a tale your thoughts could tell." The archaic syntax (a castle dark, a fortress strong) contributes to the mood of chivalry and romanticism, but it is also an indication that the composer has given prime attention to the refinement of the rhythms and cadences of the lyrics, a classical aesthetic principle. Only the artisan's careful technique informed by the artist's sensibility could have brought such a song to fruition. Again, Coppage relates the sound of the songs to the sensibilities of the composer:

> His vocals are virile in that gentlemanly, classy way our little systems are set up for. His language takes into account our long-standing prejudices toward sound and cadence (Poe made available some of his insight into this in his account of how he contrived *The Raven*: 'L'-sounds and 'R'-sounds are naturally pleasing to us, and so forth). Lightfoot's music is similarly structured within traditional feelings about which way lies man's 'higher' potential, for beauty, enlightenment, cleanliness, etc., all of which, one hopes, work out to melodies fit for kings.

The songs on *Old Dan's Records* are an example of abundant evidence for Coppage's argument. The songs are so carefully conceived that the album has a sense of uncommon artistry and accomplishment. The prettiest song on the album is "Mother of a Miner's Child." It combines, for the last time in Lightfoot's works to date, the poignant mix of the nobility of manual work and domestic love; it is set to a tune that is among Lightfoot's most simple and refined.

While Lightfoot has treated song-writing as a craft, this has not prevented him from occasionally crossing over to pop. Lightfoot has dabbled in the pop idiom almost from the beginning of his career. Interestingly, Coppage points to Lightfoot's pop tendencies as a factor in the slightly detached narrative stance characteristic of Lightfoot's songs:

> The intervals of our traditional folk melodies are — compared to the slippin', slurrin', oozin', slidin' that some other folks like in a melody — rather formal and impersonal in their prettiness. Noticing this, perhaps subconsciously, we tend to make it worse by bringing in something like a swirl of strings to warm things up. Lightfoot started doing that when he encountered John Simon, producer of his third album, *Did She Mention My Name?*, and has been tinkering with it fairly regularly since. The timeless themes and grand schemes he often tackles also tend to impose a stylized, depersonalized tone between artist and listener.

But the use of strings is not the only concession to pop — which, according to Coppage, renders myth a bit more palatable, even marketable — on the album. A song called "I

Want to Hear It from You," features brass riffs, in the style of Herb Alpert, and weepy lyrics: "Let me know how you feel/ You've got to make up your mind/ Tell me where can I run/ When my roof tumbles in?" Significantly, one of the songs on *Did She Mention My Name?*, "The Last Time I Saw Her," was for many years one of Lightfoot's favourite songs. Until *Sundown*, however, Lightfoot's interest in popularizing his music was an occasional one only.

With the release of *Sundown*, Lightfoot began to try to incorporate elements of pop and rock more or less consistently. It is not an easy transition to make. You have to be sure of what audience you are leaving behind and which one you hope to find. For Lightfoot, the attempt has been only partially successful, measured in terms of record sales. Still, because of Lightfoot's commitment to taste and restraint and all things balanced, there is no album in the Lightfoot *oeuvre* that fails completely. All the songs have that sure touch of creative care and craft. This is the way he has always worked. In 1975, when he was asked by *Canadian Composer* writer Penelope Ross how his music had been changing, he said that the process of change, for him, is a difficult one: "What I've been trying to do is to refine my writing, to get rid of the everyday approach to things, to be original without resorting to all sorts of tricks. So any growing process that I go through comes purely from writing better songs, higher quality, with more meaning, more appealing melodies. Just general improvement is all I'm after, and in order to do that, I don't have to resort to anything other than my own intellect and creative capacity."

Though the practice of trying to "poeticize" pop lyrics can often lead to dubious results, the sound and rhythm of Lightfoot's lyrics provide for interesting examinations. Much of the brilliance of Lightfoot's lyrics is to be found in the sheer sound and rhythm of his words. *East of Midnight*, for example, features such delights as, "I've been all the way to Biscayne Bay/ And all the way back again" and "Put me somewhere east of midnight,/ Along about daylight./ Anywhere I wander is where I'll take my rest." Similarly, in "If You Could Read My Mind," the alliterative use of t's in the second line, when contrasted with the first line, which has no t's, makes for very "musical" lyrics: "If you could read my mind, love/ What a tale my thoughts could tell."

As well, like all able poets, Lightfoot can write verse that speaks of one thing while referring to another parallel event or idea. The words to "Biscuit City" (from *Salute*) provide an example of Lightfoot's marvelous ability to use allegory, without losing the emotional momentum a good popular song requires. The rhythm and cadence of the verse simply ache to be spoken or sung: "I'd like to be in Biscuit City with my banjo in my hands/ I don't need no long vacation in some foreign land/ Because the sound of my own breathing has been turning to a sigh/ I wish that I could make the time to be in Biscuit City by and by." I don't know if there is a real Biscuit City — it *sounds* like somewhere in Florida — but in the song, the place takes on imaginative power. It's the "land of milk and honey," the place where domestic love has been rejuvenated: "All the girls are in bikinis/ All the boys are in the buff/ With the baby in between/ And that makes three of us."

In the spirit of true craftsmanship, Lightfoot has been slow to incorporate anything that would detract from the clarity of his musical ideas. A craftsman will not change for the sake of change. Most of Lightfoot's songs do not require much more than a simple arrangement and accompaniment. For many years, Lightfoot eschewed the use of electric instruments. His arrangements typically featured a strummed or picked acoustic guitar. With the release of *Sundown* (1974), the electric and steel guitars became more integral to the arrangements. Also, on two cuts — "Is There Anyone Home" and "Seven Island Suite" — Gene Martynec, who produced and played on Bruce Cockburn's albums for many years, plays synthesizer.

Lightfoot's vocal style has changed just as gradually as his arrangements. His voice has always been the main focus of his musical efforts. Lightfoot repeatedly refers to the "lyrical" characteristic of his voice. *Lyrical* is not often used to describe the sound of a voice, but it is clear what he's getting at: the words to a Lightfoot song must be sung to be heard. The music is a framing device, although an integral one. Lightfoot's baritone is capable of great tenderness and subtlety, even in the high range, as is apparent on the high notes on "Softly" (from *The Way I Feel*). However, most of the time it remains in the middle range.

On *East of Midnight* (1986), Lightfoot continues a tendency to deliver his vocals with less emphasis on consonants, more on vowels. The effect is conjured most effectively on "A Passing Ship"; it was first noticeable on "Knotty Pine" on *Salute* (1983). It creates an eerie sense that his voice is somehow disconnected from anything else, that it has taken on a life of its own in the song. Throughout *Salute*, in fact, Lightfoot's vocal delivery complements the allegorical and metaphorical nature of the songs. "Whispers of the North" provides a good example of this. There is a nasal tone, with an emphasis on vowels and an eccentric drawing out of certain consonants. The *th* sound in "north" and "forth" is given an unusual emphasis. For someone formally trained, the vocal sound on *Salute* cannot be attributed to bad habits or ignorance — these sounds are consciously created effects.

Aside from these vocal effects, "Whispers of the North" evokes a sense of isolation and mystery by the sound of a loon at the beginning of the song — likely chosen on the basis of personal inspiration, since Lightfoot regularly canoes and camps in the north — and by the use of a small male back-up ensemble humming a haunting riff between verses and accompanied by a pipe organ sound. There is also the use of reflexive lyrics, those words that turn the song in on itself: "The river is the melody/ The sky is the refrain." It is a remarkable song. It shows — contrary to what some critics have suggested — that Lightfoot's creative growth, while perhaps having slowed since 1978, is far from over. His ability to transform experience — in this case that of travelling by canoe through the north — into poetic myth is undiminished.

Balancing Art and Commerce

In spite of his musical reputation, Lightfoot has often been disappointed with the sales of his albums, especially the more recent ones. He has also expressed frustration about the limited promotion he thinks his record label provides for his releases, a sentiment he has given vent to since 1965, when he was bitterly disappointed with the promotion of his first two albums. Because of this, after the release of *East of Midnight*, he was quoted as saying that he would never record again. *East of Midnight* combines the sophisticated production and Lightfoot style that was so successful on *Sundown*. The music for "Anything for Love," which was written in collaboration with Canadian producer and composer David Foster, could be a lesson in pop song-writing. Structurally, it is extraordinarily tight: the "seams" are almost imperceptible. Without the lyrics by Lightfoot, the song might have been just another slick Foster production. It remains the most commercial song Lightfoot has ever released. He says today that he was indeed "going for a hit" when he recorded the song, although it garnered only a respectable amount of radio air-play in 1986.

In keeping with his commitment to Canadian folklore and legend, Lightfoot has always lived in Canada. He has expressed the alienation of living elsewhere, in "Cold Hands from New York." Unlike other Canadian singer-songwriters, Lightfoot has said that the CRTC's Canadian content regulations have not helped him. He says he sees himself as competing internationally, not just with other Canadians. Therefore, the thirty per cent Canadian content requirement on AM radio is not, according to him, of benefit. In fact, he has said that such regulations could actually hurt him, by "overexposing" his music and shortening his career. However, after the release of *Endless Wire* in 1978, the coverage of Lightfoot's career seemed to begin to dry up. *High Fidelity*, for example, lamented that the album snapped "a long string of superlative records." Until the release of *East of Midnight* in 1986, many major popular music periodicals ignored his releases. Lightfoot's transition to a rock beat and sound — as exemplified on songs such as "Hangdog Hotel Room" and "Sometimes I Don't Mind" — was not commercially successful. Lightfoot's albums during this period were continually ending up in the "delete" bin, with the characteristic puncture through the top left-hand corner.

His company, Early Morning Productions, which is based in Toronto, ensures that Lightfoot does only what he wants to do, when he wants. "I just do not do everything that comes to me," he said when I spoke with him. "It's my right and privilege as a human being." He divides his career between practice, concerts and environmental events, which he works on with broadcaster David Suzuki. His environmental work must attract a good deal of attention from those who have a stake in such matters: when I attended a Lightfoot concert in Ottawa, I sat beside an Environment Canada official (someone in "corporate communications") who was there to see what Lightfoot was up to.

That concert took place in November 1988, at the National Arts Centre in Ottawa. I heard "If You Could Read My Mind" live for the first time and felt thankful for the opportunity. Other great myth-making efforts such as "The Wreck of the Edmund Fitzgerald" have to be heard live to convey their full power. But though I had read and heard that Lightfoot could be uncongenial in concert, I was not prepared for the personal distance Lightfoot set up between himself and the audience. His banter was off-hand and half-hearted; at the end of the show, he played one encore, but waved a gesture of dismissal when the audience wanted more. The day after, the review in the *Citizen* said Lightfoot seemed "almost surprised by the fact that he was on stage doing a show."

Myth and Mythmaker

Still, Lightfoot is the only one of Canada's singer-songwriters with universal appeal. While Joni Mitchell and Neil Young have a comparably strong following and reputation, their music does not appeal to such a large number of people. While not *everyone* has heard "Circle Game" or "Heart of Gold," it is difficult to find someone who has not heard "If You Could Read My Mind," even if the version is by someone other than Lightfoot himself. Lightfoot's songs have been covered by such artists as Bob Dylan, Jerry Lee Lewis, Johnny Cash, Elvis Presley, Barbra Streisand and Glen Campbell.

Yet Canadians want their stars to be gracious and modest, to maintain a public profile for the benefit of their audiences; they expect their rich and famous to put their careers in *perspective*. (Wayne Gretzky has preserved the affections of Canadians by taking this fact to heart.) In the 1970s, Lightfoot expressed a fear of discussing his songs. He is quoted by Ritchie Yorke: "The trouble is that it's impossible to describe my art. That's why I stopped doing [interviews]. I just can't say anything about my work. I can't explain my music. Although I'm completely wrapped up in it and think about it almost all the time, even I can't describe it. You just have to listen to it for yourself, and understand it for what it is." However, after a period of crotchety appearances and a low public profile, Lightfoot seems to have turned a corner. He now grants publicity interviews, especially when touring. Perhaps such a change of heart could be interpreted as being a sign of a *lack* of modesty, rather than the opposite. But Lightfoot does not become more famous by appearing in public: his name is already very well known in Canada. Agreeing to raise his profile is a concession to his audience.

If all of this sounds like a recitation of the life of a mythical figure (or even a saint), that is appropriate. For how else but through the telling and retelling of a story can a myth be born? In Canada, Louis Riel, the Bluenose, Norman Bethune, and the building of the railroad are myths. The nobility of their stories cannot be fully conveyed in a single, authoritative version, so their stories have been told and retold until they have come to form part of the soul of the nation. In contrast, the stories of the Group of Seven, Sir John A. Macdonald or Banting and Best, despite their comparative importance and influence, do not inspire the same awe. They lack mystery. Gordon Lightfoot? Yes, he has become a Canadian myth.

But he is also a craftsman of Canadian myth. The themes of the majesty of nature, the nobility of love and the consequences of hubris are enough to sustain his work. And they may help to explain Lightfoot's remarkable ability to stay the same, stylistically, for so long, while continually writing fresh and evocative material and, as a consequence, maintaining a faithful audience. The beauty of the best of his songbook — which includes, for example, "Canadian Railroad Trilogy," "Early Morning Rain," "If You Could Read My Mind," "Sundown," "The Circle Is Small" and "Shadows"—is inscrutable.

One of the remarkable aspects of Lightfoot's life was his conviction, at a young age, that the vocation and art of songwriting were worthy of his efforts and ones to which he could commit himself for life. There is beauty and terror in the clarity with which Lightfoot regarded his calling. He has spoken of singing himself to sleep as a child, of slipping into a state of perpetual depression in adolescence, and of the ecstasy of musical expression. The fruits of his conviction have become a permanent part of Canadian mythology, for no other similar body of work in Canada can approach Lightfoot's songbook for its breadth and richness. And just as Lightfoot today recalls with warmth the childhood experience of singing the songs of Stephen Foster, perhaps another generation will recall standing on the stage of the school auditorium with the rest of the class singing "The Canadian Railroad Trilogy" and "The Long River." How else can a myth live on?

Gordon Lightfoot — The Best

Song: "If You Could Read My Mind"

Album: *Lightfoot*

Article for further reading: Tom Hopkins, "Gordon's Song: Portrait of the Artist as a No-Longer-Young Man," *Maclean's*, May 1, 1978.

Discography

Lightfoot (1965)
The Way I Feel (1967)
Did She Mention My Name? (1968)
Back Here on Earth (1968)
Sunday Concert [live] (1969)
Sit Down Young Stranger [If You Could Read My Mind] (1970)
Summer Side of Life (1971)
Don Quixote (1972)
Old Dan's Records (1972)
Sundown (1974)
Cold on the Shoulder(1975)
Gord's Gold [compilation] (1975)
Summertime Dream (1976)
Endless Wire(1978)
Dream Street Rose (1980)
Shadows (1982)
Salute (1983)
East of Midnight (1986)
Gord's Gold Volume II [compilation] (1988)

2·Chapter and Verse: Leonard Cohen

They'll never, they'll never ever reach the moon
At least not the one that we're after.
— "Sing Another Song, Boys"

Leonard Cohen's place in Montreal overlooks a tiny, peaceful patch of grass and big trees called "Parc du Portugal." On a sunny afternoon, as if posing for a postcard from Paris, old men sit in the park feeding the pigeons. The shops in the area include boutiques and antique stores. The shoe stores — there must be one on every block — carry beautiful cowboy boots made of finely crafted leather, one of Cohen's indulgences. But in spite of its touch of the trendy, it is possible to *live* in this neighbourhood. There are schools and children's voices, small grocery stores and the aroma of the local bakery. The rents are affordable for families. It is busy but not bustling. It's run-down, slightly seedy, but safe at night.

It is not the neighbourhood in which Cohen grew up. Leonard Norman Cohen was born in Montreal on Sept. 21, 1934 and grew up in Montreal's wealthy Westmount. His father, an engineer who owned a clothing factory, died when Leonard was nine. Leonard attended McGill University, graduating in 1955, and Columbia University. In addition to his home in Montreal, he now has apartments in Los Angeles and Paris and on the island of Hydra in Greece. His children — a boy named Adam and a girl named Lorca, both in their teens — live with their mother, Suzanne Elrod, in Paris. He has never married.

Cohen has chosen to continue to live in Montreal, at least part of the time, because of his affection for the city. He told *Mix* magazine: "I love Montreal because I know it so well, and probably because of its particular religious/political disposition, which makes it a very intense and holy city." In fact, in an article in *Canadian Forum* in 1983, he said he credited Montreal with providing him with an eclectic taste in music and literature: "It's because the cultures are distinct. You're taking something from the English, something from the French, something from the Jews — something from the past, something from the future. That's what makes it a good city for poets. Things are still distinct."

Cohen has taken from all of these sources — studying English literature at university (he has cited the King James Bible, Yeats, Whitman and Henry Miller as literary influences from his youth), embracing the French Catholic icons of his birthplace, and continually returning to his Jewish heritage. Any examination of his life and career inevitably involves the invocation of a multitude of names: his musical idol was Hank Williams, his literary contemporaries are William Burroughs and Jack Kerouac, and his persona as a singer owes much to Jacques Brel and Edith Piaf. Name-dropping is unavoidable in Cohen's case; as a kind of artistic junction, he cannot be separated from his many personal and artistic influences.

Actually, Leonard Cohen stands as a poetic focal point for some of Canada's most important cultural and spiritual conflicts. His inherited social standing was that of the patrician, but he seems to cherish life among immigrants, choosing to live in a former Jewish ghetto. He is a committed urbanite yet he sings about the frontier and once fancied the life of the cowboy singer. His image is alternately that of penitent and blasphemer. His sensibilities are romantic, European, literary, but he is best known as an exemplar of North American popular culture. With such rich influences and inclinations, it is no wonder academics, critics and, of course, audiences, in Canada, the US and Europe have found Cohen such a fascinating figure. Yet his commercial and artistic accomplishments have been uneven; in common with other popular musicians, he has struggled to maintain control over the creative process, with varying degrees of success.

It is the meeting of spiritual and cultural forces in Cohen's songs that provides the most fertile clue to Cohen's creative life. But first, a summary of his literary efforts. Cohen published his first book of poetry, entitled *Let Us Compare Mythologies*, in 1956. Cohen's subsequent volumes of poetry include *The Spice-Box of Earth* (1961), *Flowers for Hitler* (1964), *Parasites of Heaven* (1966), *Selected Poems* (1968), *The Energy of Slaves* (1972) and *Book of Mercy* (1984). His novels include *The Favourite Game* (1963) and *Beautiful Losers* (1966), each of which has sold approximately a million copies. *Beautiful Losers* has been translated into eleven languages. Many prominent literary figures — including Irving Layton, Louis Dudek, Allen Ginsberg and Frank Scott — have been friends and acquaintances of Cohen.

Novels and poetry were the genres that provided for Cohen the stage from which to launch his musical career. Cohen's novel *Beautiful Losers*, especially, generated a great deal of controversy and critical attention when it was published in 1966. Desmond Pacey, writing in *Canadian Literature* in 1967, called it "the most intricate, erudite and fascinating Canadian novel ever written." In 1970, Michael Ondaatje said it was "the most vivid, fascinating and brave modern novel I have read." The book follows the failures — and the paradoxical victories — of three characters: the "I" of the narrative, the narrator's wife, Edith, and his companion, named "F." It is a difficult book. The prose, while technically simple, is dense in imagery and symbolism. In the book are to be found the ideas or motives which find expression in all of Cohen's poetry and songs: the interplay of sexual and religious expression, the notion of the saint as one who has explored the borders of human possibility, and the human body as a metaphor for art and art as a metaphor for the body.

The beginning of Cohen's fame in Canada coincided with the release in 1965 of the National Film Board's *Ladies and Gentlemen, Mr. Leonard Cohen*. His first national television appearance was on CBC's *Take Thirty* in 1966. His first important public appearance as a singer was in 1967 at the Newport Folk Festival, where he appeared with other folk artists such as Joan Baez and Pete Seeger. But, as with Joni Mitchell, it took the fame and singing voice of Judy Collins to bring the focus of international popular attention to Cohen's songs: Collins recorded Cohen's "Suzanne" in 1967. In 1968 Cohen himself turned to recording, with the release that year of *Songs of Leonard Cohen*. Sales of *Songs* resulted in a reprint of *Beautiful Losers* which, in turn, led to sales of the book around the world. The year that *Songs* was released, Cohen was named the winner of the Governor General's Award for *Selected Poems* — an award which he declined to accept, stating that though he was willing, the poems would not permit it.

Sensibility of a Spiritual Cowboy

Despite the fact that Cohen's beginnings as a writer were literary, not musical, Cohen reached back to the passions of his adolescence and found that music had been associated with his concern with the written word in the past, in the form of country and western music. The cowboy, that archetype of western Canada, had been an attractive figure to Cohen for a long time. Cohen graduated from lessons in piano and clarinet to playing country music with a group called the Buckskin Boys when he was only fifteen. His intention, in fact, after returning from Greece in the early 1960s, was to become a country singer; he even bought a place near Nashville. Like Murray McLauchlan and Neil Young, Cohen plays the cowboy's instrument of choice, the harmonica. And he still wears cowboy boots (black, to match his suit).

Cohen's placement of Hank Williams at the centre of the imagery of "Tower of Song," a song from *I'm Your Man* (1988), is another indication of the cowboy's influence in Cohen's music. (Williams, who died in 1953 at the age of twenty-nine, was best known for his efforts, novel at the time, to blend country and pop.) In 1971, songs from Cohen's first album were featured on Robert Altman's film *McCabe and Mrs. Miller*, a work that has been described by film critic and historian Jack C. Ellis as "a kind of anti-Western," a fitting description of the country style Cohen has developed. The prototypical "anti-Western" Cohen song is "Fingerprints" from *Death of a Ladies' Man* — while the musical setting of a country song often calls for a recitation of lost love, *this* singer sings about the loss of identity as indicated by the loss of the physical emblems of human identity: "Fingerprints, fingerprints/ Where are you now, my fingerprints?"

In spite of his habits of solitude (he lives alone), Cohen has said he needs to be a part of contemporary society; thus his

attraction to popular music. The original mode he chose for
the expression of that attraction is telling, however. He chose
what he considered the most "authentic" of popular music's
idioms: country music. At the time, in the early 1960s, he was
unaware that there were others — Bob Dylan, Phil Ochs, Judy
Collins and Joan Baez — who were trying to find in their
musical efforts the accomplishment of the same ends. It is an
artistic stance that he has affirmed repeatedly in his life. He is
serious about his writing and expends a great deal of energy
working on it. It receives critical acclaim, in varying degrees
of intensity. But Cohen also feels that his work must remain
accessible to a larger audience: thus, the song-writing and the
performing, the novels and the interviews, the ascetic lifestyle
and the carefully cultivated image.

In the tradition of the cowboy, Cohen's aesthetic image has
been that of a romantic. Yet Cohen's romanticism is, like so
much of his verse and lyrics, a subtle form of parody, as critic
Bart Testa points out: "It's a kind of romanticism in reverse.
Romanticism is leaving religion to find it in nature; Leonard
Cohen leaves nature to find it in a kind of fetid, somewhat
perverse eroticism within the space of religion." Accordingly,
Cohen onstage looks like either a priest or a turtle. He has also
been called "Christ-like." Here is a description of one of his
New York performances, as reported in *Rolling Stone*: "Dressed
in a double-breasted black suit, Cohen — calm, pale and intense — looked like both penitent and preacher as he bent or
kneeled to the ground to lay down or raise up his black guitar
or a glass of water after each number." His appearance as a
penitent is appropriate to his disposition.

Part of Cohen's interest in religion is a result of his search
for a language that encompasses all human concerns. For
Cohen, the language of theology is all-inclusive in a way that
no other language can be. Thus, Cohen's volume of poetry
entitled *Book of Mercy* retains the tone and imagery of the
Psalms. It deals with human love, death, rage and spirituality,
all within a context of reverence that lends it authority. Because mercy is the prerogative of the divine, although it often
passes through human channels, a sense of spirituality per-
vades the book. Commenting on *Book of Mercy*, Cohen has said,
"We have perceptions that go beyond our ordinary faculties
of perception — beyond the rational — and that is the area of

prayer. It defies or challenges the ordinary apparatus by which we operate. But it is verifiable, discernible, and I don't think anybody can ignore it indefinitely."

Cohen's interest in Christ is related to his view that the teacher must not be isolated from his followers, as he told *Melody Maker*:

> I always liked the founder of Christianity.... His moral stance is unequalled — he's the only guy who's put himself squarely with the outcast, with the leper, with the sinner, with the prostitute, with the criminal. Nobody is excluded from his embrace. There have been some startling religious figures, but I don't think there's anybody who said so specifically that *nobody* is beyond this embrace. It's so subversive and so revolutionary that we haven't even begun to deal with it. It's a miracle those ideas have lasted in the world, because there's no evidence that the meek shall inherit the earth.

But Cohen's embrace of religion is dialectical: his Jewish heritage, for example, cannot be separated from his identity as a Montrealer, surrounded as he is by the Catholic monuments of Quebec's history. As Testa points out: "He's managed to be syncretistic about his Jewish guilt. He's one of the few people who's managed to turn Jewish guilt into Catholic eroticism. That's a pretty good trick, even for a really good poet." Thus, Cohen's imagery often borrows from the Bible. Prominent in this imagery is the figure of Christ himself, who, as Cohen told *Musician* magazine, is the "perfect symbol for our civilization," citing what he sees as the imperative of the death of the individual's personality in modern Western life.

Catholicism, of course, was the first institution to be established by Europeans in New France. Cohen has not escaped its grasp. And though he is a resident of the "New World," Cohen appeals to audiences in the "Old World" as well. In fact, he has a larger audience in Europe than he does in North America. *Various Positions* sold 300,000 copies in Europe but was not even released in the US. Cohen's following in Poland is extraordinary (there is a Cohen festival each year in Krakow). Before martial law was declared in Poland, a Solidarity official requested that Cohen appear at a union rally in Warsaw. Cohen follows the European tradition of Jacques Brel and Piaf — singers whose ability to portray their personality was more important than their ability to write or sing. In this kind of performance the conjuring of style is as important as the content of the songs. In a moment of flippancy, Cohen explained his popularity in Europe by the fact that Europeans don't understand the lyrics. Another time, however, he said, "I think the public world in Europe is not as powerful as the public world here, so there's still an inner space that's not so much under assault. There's still some remnant of nineteenth-century culture."

The Poet and the Pop Star

Cohen does not have the spontaneous and dynamic presence that other popular musicians have and which has come to be expected in North America. This is another clue to his relative popularity in Europe. In live performance, Cohen sings with less melodic interest than he does on his albums. In the recording studio he can choose from among several takes; in concert he tries to highlight the drama of his personal presence by putting less emphasis on musical interest. On a fall 1989 episode of the television program *Night Music*, for example, he sang "Tower of Song" with almost no bodily movement, his expression trance-like, and in a kind of wavering bass monotone. Any musical interest was provided by the tinkling riffs he played on his electronic keyboard. At the end of the song, he slowly walked back and stood between the two young women who were singing background vocals. The three of them turned and walked up a flight of steps at the back of the set. It was the kind of marvelous dramatic play by which Cohen establishes the ceremonial moment of his performances.

On the other hand, Cohen has never claimed to possess immense musical powers, either as an instrumentalist or as a singer. He is one of those artists who turn to music in the hope that they will find the acceptance they cannot find in other disciplines. He was perhaps the first of the performance artists who have found a niche in the artistic world by straddling visual art and music. By composing songs, instead of poems, he has been able to avoid the verdict of academe. He refuses to accede to the assumption that virtuosity is a prerequisite for musical achievement. Still, Cohen often talks about song-writing as a craft, as he did when he was interviewed for *Music Scene* magazine in 1971:

>I don't have these dramatic, extravagant feelings about my works. I try to do my work. If it's in the books for me to stay on the crust of this star for a long time, I'll keep doing what I'm doing to the best of my ability. I don't see one moment (of inspiration) as any big climax. It's just a matter of sharpening your tools, keeping in shape, of wholesome discipline, surprise, adventure — things that keep your strength — but not to have the notion that there's one moment and there's going to be a white light and everything will turn into dust.

Cohen is the only successful Canadian popular musician to have incorporated the European folk musical influence in his music. For as much as any of the others can be called eclectic, only a Cohen song could have an accompaniment with a flamenco flavour such as the one heard on "Avalanche," from *Songs of Love and Hate*. Thus, Cohen represents the "old world" sensibilities that have been largely abandoned in the English Canadian mainstream. His mother, a Russian who lived through the Revolution, provided for him the European sense of proximity to and involvement with the past. As a committed resident of Montreal, the capital of the cradle of Canada (New France, or Quebec, was, after all, the first European community to be established in Canada), he absorbed the sense of the Old World (as distinct from the Old Country) that is not as evident elsewhere in Canada.

Cohen's literary efforts, too, display the European influence. In an article in *Canadian Literature* in 1967, Sandra Djwa placed Cohen the novelist and poet in the tradition of the Black Romantics. That tradition is rooted in Europe in the poetry of Baudelaire, whose "flowers of evil" are an interesting contrast to the "favourite game" (from Cohen's novel of the same name), which involved making flower-like imprints in the snow with the body. The Black Romantic's art is an expression of his exploration and experience of evil: "The modern anti-hero accepts evil as part of existence and immerses himself within it, both in terms of the external world and through the journey into self. This immersion in destruction, often accomplished through a combination of alcohol, drugs and sex, would seem to be metaphysical in nature in that it is an attempt to find a new answer to the human predicament by going down instead of up." The objective in immersing oneself in the abyss is to find a "new revelation."

In terms of both subject and technique, Cohen's novels are often compared to the best known American exemplar of the Black Romantic tradition, William Burroughs. Like Cohen's, Burroughs' work has been released fitfully and remains relatively slim. Parallels between *Beautiful Losers* and Burroughs' experimental novel *Naked Lunch* are not hard to find: a fearless treatment of sexual concerns, the use of the "cut-up" technique of composition, a cinematic feel to the "narrative," and an opaque plot line. Both authors suffered — or enjoyed — a great deal of controversy and criticism with the release of their books.

Naked Lunch, published in 1959, became a landmark case in censorship law in the US. It was apparently the last literary work to be censored by the post office, the Customs Service and a state government. Burroughs was a member of the Beats, a group of writers who opposed most powers of government, avoided traditional institutions, and used narcotics of almost any kind, and who were considered the forerunners of the North American counterculture of the 1960s. Burroughs, along with the other two most famous of the Beats — Allen Ginsberg and Jack Kerouac — shook up the literary sensibilities of the 1950s and 1960s and influenced a generation of writers and poets, including rock lyricists such as Mike Jagger and, in Canada, Bruce Cockburn. Both Burroughs and Cohen use the decay of literary form to reflect the decay of traditional social and moral authority. While Burroughs fashioned a writing technique he called "cut-up," in which newspapers, novels, the writer's own writing, and anything else at hand were spliced more or less randomly, Cohen's technique is "pure list," as Djwa has put it. The result in both authors' work is a disjointed anti-narrative that most readers find difficult and disorienting.

As for the lyrics of his songs, however, Cohen has named a European, the Spanish poet Federico Garcia Lorca (1898-1936), as a strong influence. Lorca's personal background was strikingly similar to Cohen's. Like Cohen, Lorca practised more than just the poet's art: he was also a composer, pianist, guitarist, painter and dramatist. Also in common with Cohen, he was well-educated and came from a wealthy family. Furthermore, religious imagery informed all of his art; Catholicism was an important formative influence in his life. Both Lorca and Cohen studied law and literature; in fact, both attended

Columbia although, of course, Cohen was there much later.
Finally, they share a mystical view of human relationships,
especially those between men and women. For Lorca's part,
he felt a kind of kinship with his father's first wife, who had
died before marrying Federico's mother. In other words, he
was intrigued by the woman who *might* have been his mother.
Most importantly, however, one of Lorca's main themes is the
freedom of the individual, especially as it is expressed in sex-
uality. The following lines from Lorca's early poem "Sleep-
walking Ballad" could be Cohen's as well: "Green how I want
you green. Green wind. Green branches."

The academic community has found it difficult to ignore
Cohen. As one of the most published poets of the mid-1960s
in Canada, he was considered a "phenomenon" in Canadian
letters: his youth, boldness and then-prolific output made for
a stunning debut as a public figure. In 1967, *Canadian Literature*
devoted an issue to the theme of "Views of Leonard Cohen."
He is regularly anthologized as not only a Canadian but as one
of the world's finest contemporary poets. Canadian literary
critics Dennis Lee and Stephen Scobie have each written a
book on Cohen's work, *Savage Fields* and *Leonard Cohen*, respectively. Cohen holds an honorary doctor of laws degree from
Dalhousie University. In spite of all of this interest in his literary work, publication slowed after the release of *The Energy of
Slaves* in 1972. Since then, he has released only two volumes,
Death of a Lady's Man and *Book of Mercy*.

Poet and literary critic George Bowering, writing in
Canadian Literature, called Cohen the "ultimate lyric man": "He
shows any range of his discoveries, mundane to metaphysical,
always through his consciousness of singular self." For such a
sensibility, what could be a better choice than to become a
popular singer-songwriter? In no other genre of art is the first
person narrative point of view considered sacred. And Cohen
has said, recently, that he has resigned himself to being a
singer-songwriter: "Now I know what I am. I'm not a novelist.
I'm not the light of my generation. I'm not the spokesman for
new sensibility. I'm a songwriter living in LA, and this is my
new record."

Not surprisingly, Cohen's imagery and themes overlap
among all the genres he was worked in. For example, while
"Tower of Song" features the motive of the predicament of the

songwriter, which is common to Cohen's other songs, its image of the speaker addressing the audience from a tower is borrowed from the last paragraph of *Beautiful Losers*; a "lonely wooden tower" appears in the song "Suzanne" as well. The lyrics of "Tower of Song" reveal a singer whose sense of self has been destroyed: the singer has "no choice" and is imprisoned by his audience. Again, the theme of the loss of self can be found throughout Cohen's literary work, but especially in *Beautiful Losers*, as Stephen Scobie points out: "The merging of all the characters at the end of *Beautiful Losers* into one indistinguishable whole is only the final extension of a tendency visible throughout Cohen's work."

I suppose a simple list of Cohen's created works might suggest that Cohen is more literary figure than pop legend. In fact, Cohen has devoted most of his creative energy to propagating popular culture as a whole. In interviews, while Cohen usually does not talk generally about music, when he does, it becomes clear just how well he has assimilated popular culture, a sphere in which popular music is the dominant force. A rare insight of this type is to be found in an interview with him conducted in 1988 by Mark Rowland of *Musician* magazine. Noting first that musical criticism is based on principles that were common in the nineteenth century, typified by the aphorism that "I know what I like," Cohen goes to the heart of the phenomenon of popular music since 1960: "People talk about me being a primitive, they use 'folk singer' as a way to put people down, things like that. I'm a folk singer, okay, but I mean, some folk singer wrote the melody to 'Greensleeves'. How primitive was that? Nobody is identifying our popular singers like a Matisse or Picasso. Dylan's a Picasso — that exuberance, range, an assimilation of the whole history of music."

Still, the way Cohen writes sets him apart from many other popular composers. For him, the process of writing — whether a song or poem — is one of paring and leaving aside, of writing and rewriting, of trying to find the right poetic stance. He has said he works on his songs one word at a time. Two songs from *I'm Your Man*, for example, started out as much more ambitious pieces than their final versions. The title track was about waiting for a miracle, then turned into a song in which the singer talks to himself about his yearning for a lover. Similarly,

"I Can't Forget" was in its nascent form a hymn to personal exodus, with the Jewish flight from bondage as the metaphor. It became simply a song about a moment of personal crisis. Cohen's lyrics, like the residences he keeps, are spare and economical. As a result, his output over the years has been relatively slim. However, the gems of his career remain: "Who By Fire," "Hallelujah," "Tower of Song," and the best known of them all, "Suzanne."

The Spector of Death

In spite of his acceptance of the role of popular musician, Cohen has resisted some of the trappings and exigencies of the popular music industry. He doesn't live the life of the pop legend. Instead, he has chosen austerity over excess in his personal life and has released albums only when he feels they are ready, artistically, to be released. However, *Death of a Ladies' Man* (1977) provides an exception to this. It is an example of the dangers of acquiescing to the currents of the popular music industry.

Cohen worked on the album with the venerable producer Phil Spector. Even as the album was being released, Cohen himself was expressing dissatisfaction with the result. Critics were even more harsh: *Village Voice* called the album "an embarrassingly turgid disappointment." The importance for a popular composer of maintaining control over the recording process is demonstrated in the fiasco of *Death of a Ladies' Man*. Spector chose the tracks to be used in the album and mixed them at a secret location. As a result, the songs, according to Cohen, lost their "guts." Cohen has said that he was hoping to find Spector in his "Debussy" stage but found him, instead, in his "Wagnerian" one. With *Death of a Ladies' Man*, the songs became melodramatic, maudlin. It was as if Cohen was beginning to parody himself.

Cohen has found it difficult to take control of the entire creative process the way Joni Mitchell and Neil Young, for example, have been able to do, in the face of commercial pressure to be, instead, controlled by it. They treat technical aspects of the recording process, such as the mix, as part of the composition process.

With the beginning of recording technology, performances were recorded live, perhaps several times in order to provide a choice among renditions. Today, many "tracks" are recorded separately, each track featuring an instrument or voice. The musicians maintain a consistent tempo among the tracks by wearing earphones through which the beats of a metronome may be heard. In the early days of recording, four tracks was considered enough. Today, sixty-four or more tracks may be used. When the producer and the composer have decided enough "takes" of each musical part have been recorded, they mix the tracks onto a master tape, which is used, in turn, for copying to LP disc, compact disc or cassette. The mixing stage is critical because it determines how loud an instrument or voice will be heard, if at all, and because the volume and the equalization (the relative prominence of high and low frequencies) can be changed dramatically at this stage. In addition, various effects can be introduced, such as reverberation or the doubling of voices.

Phil Spector had become a millionaire by the age of twenty-one by taking a fresh approach to producing popular albums: he treated the mixing process as a part of the overall creative process. Before Spector's era, record companies released as many songs as they could, as quickly as possible, in the hope that a few would become hits. In the early 1960s, Spector produced hit after hit by spending a great deal of time dubbing, overdubbing, and rerecording the various musical components of a recording. The result was a distinctive sound that the record-buying public found attractive, heard in such hits as "Be My Baby" by the Ronettes and "You've Lost that Lovin' Feelin'" by the Righteous Brothers. In film language, Spector adopted the role of the *auteur*, creating the "Spector sound." It changed the way members of the music industry thought about recruiting talent, recording, distribution, marketing and promotion. In the case of *Death of a Ladies' Man* — whether as a result of temperament or aptitude — Cohen allowed Spector to determine the final artistic result. He has since complained bitterly about it.

Melding Music and the Written Word: "Suzanne"

The travails of *Death of a Ladies' Man*, which represent the low point of Cohen's commercial success, do not dim the lustre of his greatest achievements such as "Suzanne," his best known and most beautiful song. Released on *Songs of Leonard Cohen* in 1967, literary critic Stephen Scobie has written that in the song all the "loneliness and pain of the beautiful loser is transmuted into joy." In it the influences and traditions I have discussed are powerfully expressed.

The images in the lyrics are economically presented. They can be considered in a few cohesive groups: water, river and mirror; sun and orange; sailors, heroes and children; garbage, flowers and seaweed. The song reveals that Cohen understood very clearly, even at the beginning of his musical career, the necessities of transcription from poetry to song. In the first verse, for example, there are pairs of rhyming line ends, largely absent in Cohen's poetry (river/forever, blind/mind) and rhymes internal to the line (tell her/give her). Furthermore, a chorus is repeated after every verse, a device alien to Cohen's poetry. Even so, the chorus for the second verse is written for "him" (Jesus) rather than for "her" (Suzanne), allowing a variation that is deliciously disconcerting for a popular song. In an interview in *Canadian Forum* in 1983, Cohen talked about the difference between writing lyrics for a song and writing poetry:

> When you're working with just a printed text, whatever gestalt you convey has to be within the flesh of the syntax. You won't have the guitar to move the words along. It's like placing things in aspic: They live on the pages — the words and phrases — and they have to be written with that in mind. The ideas and emotions are not fluid in the sense that a song is. They have a kind of rhythm and authority, but it's a different kind of process. But I like to make sure that my lyrics stand an examination on the page.

In spite of the poetic richness of "Suzanne," it is difficult to think of how a popular song could be simpler in its chord progressions or melody. Significantly, the song does not follow the standard twelve-bar blues pattern characteristic of many popular songs of this period. Still, the chord changes follow a slow ascent to and descent from a peak in the same way that a twelve-bar blues pattern does. Some harmonic interest is compensated for by the use of four chords in the harmonic progression (G, A minor, B minor and C) instead of three. The peak of the progression occurs, in the first verse, at the phrase "all the way from China," and, in the chorus, at the phrase "want to travel blind." The melody consists of only six notes, some repeated.

A common criticism of popular music is that it doesn't last, that its subject-matter and its musical and lyrical forms are too limited to allow it to wear very well. This criticism can be applied to much of popular musicians' output, but certainly not all. While "Billy Don't Be a Hero" is lost among all the other songs that mistook sentimentality for significant emotion, "Suzanne" bears listening more than twenty years after it was written. Of Cohen's most recent songs, "Tower of Song" will likely enjoy the same kind of longevity as "Suzanne."

Various critics have attempted to sort out the lyrical and musical strands of "Suzanne" and to explain its luminous attraction. The song's central mystery remains intact, of course. It may be interesting and even intellectually and emotionally edifying to know some of the biographical details that shed light on some of the phrases: Cohen's own mental demons ("you know that she's half crazy"), the Black Romantic's metaphor of the poet's ravaged body for the poetry itself ("But he himself was broken"), and even the archetype of the "beautiful loser" from Cohen's second novel ("There are heroes in the seaweed.")

But after enumerating this catalogue of images and facts, I have come no further in explaining the *experience* of listening to "Suzanne" than I was when I sat in a friend's apartment one afternoon, cup of tea in hand, and listened to it, breathless, for the first time — knowing nothing about Cohen's life, works or sensibilities. The simple accompaniment on acoustic guitar and the childlike voice — Cohen's voice has become lower over the years — were part of the emotional effect it had on me, but only one part. And that is the mystery of a popular song masterpiece. Taken separately, the several aspects of the song (the lyrics, the music and accompaniment, the performance itself) may be quite unremarkable. Taken together, they can create an emotional synergy for the listener that defies critical analysis. "Suzanne" has lasted a couple of decades: as long as there is a Montreal, a people living there intensely conscious of their past, and a body of religious and historical relics confronting them daily, "Suzanne" will endure.

Leonard Cohen — The Best

Song: "Suzanne"

Album: *I'm Your Man*

Article for further reading: Mark Rowland, "Leonard Cohen's Nervous Breakthrough," *Musician* no. 117 (July 1988): 94-8+.

Discography

Songs of Leonard Cohen (1968)
Songs from a Room (1969)
Songs of Love and Hate (1971)
Live Songs [live] (1972)
New Skin for the Old Ceremony (1973)
The Best of Leonard Cohen [compilation] (1975)
Death of a Ladies' Man (1977)
Recent Songs (1979)
Various Positions (1984)
I'm Your Man (1988)

3·My Crazy Old Uncle, Neil Young

Well I keep gettin' younger
My life's been funny that way
                              — *"Crime in the City"*

When Neil Young performed at Exhibition Stadium in Toronto in 1987, 21,000 people showed up for the occasion. Not bad for a rocker who, at the time, was forty-one years old. Nowadays, it is a strange crowd he attracts, though: teenyboppers and parents of teenyboppers. It is true that when these two groups mix, the result can be, well, generational dissonance. For Young likes to rock. His guitar playing has been compared to the disembowelling of the instrument; he plays and sings loud and hard. A friend who attended the concert, someone who *could* be a parent of a teenybopper, although he isn't, reflected on the event in a letter published in the *Globe and Mail* a couple of weeks after: "In addition to paying good money to see a wall of denim backsides, we were endangered by 850 pounds of arrhythmic flesh tottering on the wobbly fold-out chairs in front of and behind us." Yet Young has been successful in providing artistic reconciliation between the two groups. If his surname provides a clue to his personality, he is always "Young"; he is living proof that rock can continually re-create itself. As a personification of rock's identity as a phenomenon "outside of time," Young appeals to listeners of any age who are attracted by the notion of personal rebirth.

Neil Young is one of the few Canadian popular musicians who have left Canada and now enjoy international success. His consistent level of creative activity is reflected in the attention he has received in the musical press: scores of articles in *Rolling Stone, Billboard* and, of course, the music sections of daily newspapers and popular publications such as *Time*. But as part of the price of that success, Young has had to yield in some measure to the strictures of the popular music industry, and this is the central fact of his artistic and personal growth. He has made a career of challenging rock's boundaries in the same way that a composer of high art music might. This is not to suggest that Young is better for having somehow "aspired" to greater things than rock; it is simply to suggest that he stands out from his colleagues. His attitude to music is more "artistic" than theirs, in that he has consistently demonstrated his will to move on, to create anew and to take risks. In his art and in his lifestyle, Young is a romantic, choosing to trust intuition and passion over reason. If critics and journalists have appeared confused and bemused by his sometimes cagey and fitful musical efforts, virtually all have been compelled to respect him for his attempt.

While one might assume that high art composers are under more artistic constraints than popular musicians, it is in fact the other way around. The degree to which rockers can challenge or even offend their listeners is extremely limited. Lyrics, regardless of their merit, must be accessible and, above all, possessed of a "hook," a memorable musical or lyrical phrase. The reason for this is related to the nature of the medium: radio is for turning on and off; stereos, except those in the possession of audiophiles, are usually played as background to some activity other than listening to music. Also, the audience for popular music passes through a kind of revolving door. As the older listeners (say thirty-year-olds) begin to take up pursuits that do not lend themselves to the use of pop music as an aural backdrop, some of them may begin listening to other kinds of music (although some, as the audiences at Young concerts reveal, continue to support their favourite performers). As older listeners leave the audience, other listeners (say, four-teen-year-olds) enter.

Of course, demographics have made this situation more complicated than it may seem, as the advent of "classic rock" stations has shown. However, the audience for popular music remains homogeneous in that all its members have the same *use* for music — popular music, regardless of its merit, is usually background music. Witness the audience at Exhibition Stadium. Composers of high art music, on the other hand, have almost a duty to extend, delimit or challenge the bounds of their art form; not to do so can result in a reputation for not being serious — and in all that such a reputation implies, including failure to receive government grants and sponsorships.

In the career of any successful popular musician, there comes a time when he or she feels the strait-jacket of economic success: at that point, he or she must choose whether to hang on to the audience or risk losing it. This moment of truth has been most obvious in the careers of Joni Mitchell and Gordon Lightfoot, for they, along with Young, have had to confront sudden and enormous financial success. Artistically, Young has repeatedly chosen the more risky alternative. *Harvest* was the first turning point — reaching the place of number one album in the US in 1972, it represented a remarkable achievement for Young. In both unrivalled artistic and commercial success, he has never duplicated this achievement; since then, he has been successful in pursuing one kind or the other, but not both.

Rise of a Rocker

Young's "story" has been recited in countless magazine and newspaper articles and even a couple of books. Neil Percy Young was born in Toronto on Nov. 12, 1945. His father, Toronto sportswriter Scott Young, has written a book about his relationship with his son, entitled *Neil and Me*, published in 1984. Neil descends from a family of singers, farmers and one Presbyterian clergyman turned revivalist preacher, Scott Young's maternal grandfather. As Neil grew up, his life was touched by some of Canada's well-known writers, the neighbours and visitors at his family's home: Pierre Berton, Farley Mowat, June Callwood, Robertson Davies.

Young took up the guitar when he was a boy. In 1963, after stints with several bands in Winnipeg, Young began playing in a band called the Squires. The group was popular in Winnipeg and travelled to other towns in Manitoba and Ontario. Towards the end of his association with the group, Young wrote one of his most popular songs, "Sugar Mountain." The song is famous not only as one of Young's earliest songs but as the inspiration, according to Young, for Joni Mitchell's classic, "Circle Game."

The Mynah Birds, with which Young played during 1965 and 1966, got a contract to record for Motown in Detroit, but when Ricky James Matthews, another member of the band, was incarcerated for deserting the US Navy, the band broke up. In March of 1966, Buffalo Springfield was formed in California by Young, Bruce Palmer, Stephen Stills, Richie Furay and Dewey Martin. The band's popularity, based on songs that included Young's "Burned" and "Out of My Mind," lasted until 1968, when the members went their separate ways. But the band's reputation and accomplishments have followed Young ever since. Buffalo Springfield albums are still commercially available. The band is one of those phenomena in popular music that gains legendary stature. Their sound, their musical style, and even their peculiarities in performance (such as Furay's habit of tip-toeing across the stage backwards while playing) seemed to resonate long after the band's dissolution. The band, like Young himself, represented a romantic effort to test rock's boundaries and conventions.

The first album recorded by Neil Young and Crazy Horse, which was formed in February 1969 and which has lasted, off and on, to the present, was *Everybody Knows This Is Nowhere*. The band has recorded several albums since then with Young. Crosby, Stills, Nash and Young (CSNY), formed in 1969, played at Woodstock (as only their second gig together) and have performed and recorded occasionally since then. As with Buffalo Springfield, CSNY achieved a level of popularity that went beyond record sales; critics and fans today still watch for the latest reunification of the group, although to date these have been without the participation of Young. CSNY broke new artistic ground, and listeners and fans have been expressing their admiration ever since. Other bands that Young has formed — for the purposes of recording and touring — are the Stray Gators, the Santa Monica Flyers, Trans Band, the Shocking Pinks, the Redwood Boys, and the International Harvesters.

Born to Run

In an interview with Canadian rock critic Ritchie Yorke, Young said that when he was a teenager, popular musicians were trying to get out of Canada and into the US so their music could be heard: "I spent some time in Toronto training myself as a folksinger. But I soon realized that nothing was ever going to happen in Toronto. I split and went to Los Angeles. I was just completely fed up with the Canadian scene." However, when he needs time to reflect, he returns to Canada. At certain times of crisis, in fact — such as when he was making up his mind to leave Crosby, Stills, Nash and Young — Young has said that he feels a need for space. Still, he says he feels at home in the US (albeit as a non-voting resident), as he stated in a 1985 interview with *Musician* magazine: "I've been all over the world and I feel at home here [in the US]. I like to move all around the whole continent. That's my place."

Aside from an occasional reference to Canadian place names, Young sings of American legend and myth, not Canadian: his symbols have included Pocahontas, space stations and the settlement of the American west. For its part, *Rolling Stone* has called him "the last American hero"; and his music has been featured among the most important contemporary American compositions in a book by music critic John Rockwell entitled *All American Music*. Furthermore, he is the only rocker I know of who plays that most American of instruments, the banjo. (It is hard to think of a more distinctly American instrument than the banjo, since the idea of strings resonating on a skin head was brought to North America by black slaves.) Other examples of his embrace of the US as his home are not hard to find. "For the Turnstiles," a song on which Young plays the banjo, is about nothing less than baseball, that mythological American amusement. Similarly, on *Everybody's Rockin'*, Young praises the glories of American rock 'n' roll, with references, in turn, to Payola, Nancy and Ronald Reagan, and Alan Freed. On the same album, he even covers "Mystery Train," the song chosen by rock critic Greil Marcus as the prototypical American rock 'n' roll song. Of course, the most famous piece of evidence of Young's adoption of the US is his song "Ohio," which was one of the anthems of the American counterculture.

The first part of Young's path as a rocker is familiar; it is a journey of romantic longing and passion, marked by a continual effort to "head out on the highway." Beginning as a member of the lower or middle class, the prototypical rocker uses his music as a means to gain some kind of leg up on his beginnings and on his environment which he sees as oppressive. After the advent of success, however, the rocker again feels caged, a victim of the system he thought he was defeating. He becomes locked in a cycle of recordings, performances and contracts. Young, on the other hand, has consistently tried — from the very act of recording *Tonight's the Night* and *Old Ways* to the seizure of almost complete control over the recording process on all his albums — to dismantle the popular music industry's systematic alienation of the audience from the artist. Young's views on this are stated most succinctly in "Prisoners of Rock 'n' Roll": "When we're jamming in our old garage/ The girls come over and it sure gets hot/ We don't want to be watered down/ Taking orders from record company clowns/ That's why we don't want to be good."

Ironically, of course, after achieving this kind of artistic freedom and direct access to his audience, Young then often offers the audience what it *doesn't* want: he takes another artistic turn just as the audience becomes settled into the previous pattern of writing and performing. It's another indication of his desire to continually break down barriers and push back boundaries. Young has said that he repeatedly experiences a compulsion to move on, musically and geographically, a process he compares metaphorically to a moth repeatedly running into a light bulb. With regard to his artistic restlessness, he takes his cue from the musicians who were formative influences in Young's early musical career — mainly the Beatles and Bob Dylan. These were musicians who were always artistically one step ahead of their last album.

For Young, the only way to remain creatively active is to abandon one's accomplishments as soon as they are completed, as he told *Musician* magazine in 1985: "After I have a big peak it seems like I don't want to be there anymore.... I just hate being labeled. I hate to be stuck in one thing. I just don't want to be anything for very long. I don't know why." Such an attitude can be frustrating for fans, who, when they attend a concert, want to hear the standards, such as "Heart of Gold," "Only Love Can Break Your Heart" and "Cinnamon Girl." During the tour to promote *Tonight's the Night*, Young played the tour's theme song — which many in the audience had never heard before — four times, prefacing each repetition with the words, "Here's a song you'll recognize." Young's artistic ramblings may be traced partly to his unwillingness to accept the stereotype he has as a proponent of the counterculture, as R.A. Hull wrote in 1981 in an article in *Creem* magazine:

> Like all immortal primitives from Bo Diddley to the Ramones, Young employs minimalism as an attack against the ennui of rock's slick tyranny. On "Ambulance Blues" and "Revolution Blues," he comes as close as he ever has to bringing Dylan's '60's revolt back home (except that, in the '70's, blowing in the wind becomes "pissing in the wind"). But to do that, he had to stand alone, which meant disavowing the counter-culture that nurtured him. It's this simple fact that has caused some to disregard Young as a wasted has-been, an ex-hippie who lost his way toward mellow unconconsciousness, yet it's also this fact that makes him probe the black landscape that so few dare even acknowledge ("still the searcher must ride the dark horse" could qualify as Young's motto), that which makes his music so truthfully alive (his critics might say sloppy, but in rock 'n' roll, that's usually the same thing).

Challenging the Boundaries of Rock

The most important album to establish Young's reputation as a major figure of the counterculture was *After the Gold Rush*. Released in 1970, it is a powerful album because of its mix of the most successful elements in Young's music to that point. The background vocals on cuts such as "Only Love Can Break Your Heart" have the passion, without the polish, of Crosby, Stills, Nash and Young. Remarkably, the album features the sixteen-year-old Nils Lofgren, who would become one of rock's great guitarists, playing the piano for the first time (he had played accordion and guitar before, but not piano); his piano playing sounds as innocent as Young's voice.

And nothing provides the Youngian imagination with more fertile ground than Young's voice. It is rock's only innocent voice. It has been called "a child's whimper begging for what may never come" by *Creem*. With its narrow dynamic range (even at the lyrics' most intense emotional moments) and its occasional intimations of sobbing, Young's voice wrenches his songs from the plane of time and space into a unique realm — with the sense that *every* voice and *no* voice is singing — that other singers can only imitate. As a result, albums such as *After the Gold Rush* bear listening even after almost two decades since their release.

Most remarkably, in a year that saw the release of so many records with so much *stuff* on them (*Jesus Christ Superstar*, for example), the album features simple arrangements that suggest a feeling of space. "After the Gold Rush," after all, is accompanied only by piano and, of all instruments, French horn. And if it is possible to pin down just what it is that propels Young's work from the realm of pop formula to that of art, the physical notion of empty space has to be considered. Almost every aspect of Young's creative life suggests it. Consider the names of the bands Young has put together, more or less singlehandedly: "Buffalo Springfield," "Crazy Horse," "Stray Gators," and "International Harvesters." The image evoked is always that of breaking loose, of heading for higher, open ground. Consider Young's one-dimensional nasal voice, which seems to repel the forces that would fill the void. Consider the album covers, which might show Young with his back to the camera or looking away (*After the Gold Rush, On the Beach, Decade*) or from a distance (*Everybody Knows This Is Nowhere*). Consider Young's trek across the continent in search of a musical frontier, much in the same way settlers a hundred years ago sought a geographical frontier. All suggest the motive of opening up, moving out, finding more room. They are visual depictions of his romantic goal of challenging artistic boundaries.

One of the ironies of the folksinger-songwriter is that he or she must not only reveal his or her personality but also create a sense of the *other* in the act of creative expression. In trying to achieve universal appeal, the folksinger must set up the illusion that he speaks — and sings — for all; this while appearing "sincere," that most prized of folk qualities. Young's quest for direct communication, honesty and identification with "the folk" later in his career led him to explore the country music idiom more intensively. But the triptych of *Time Fades Away, On the Beach,* and *Tonight's the Night* (released, respectively, in 1973, 1974 and 1975) best illustrates Young's determination to somehow experience the subterranean sources of human experience and thereby communicate directly with his audience. Again, Young wanted to see how far he could push artistically. He was enacting the romantic desire for dramatic change, movement, raw emotion. These albums have the unmistakable air of the artist's descent into hell. They were among Young's least commercially successful.

Perhaps more than any other popular musician, Young has chronicled the story of the drug culture in North America. *Time Fades Away, On the Beach, Tonight's the Night* tell the individual and collective story of the advent of widespread use of hallucinogens in society. His interest in the drug culture may, again, be considered in relation to his interest in new frontiers and in the romantic struggle for individuality. For many of those who experimented with drugs in the 1960s and 1970s, drugs offered a means of discovery. For Young, the phenomenon was yet another sphere in which he could challenge boundaries. Young's commentary on and testament to the drug culture began as early as his Buffalo Springfield days. "Out of My Mind," for example, is about not only the demons of success and rock stardom but also the psychedelic experiences that, for Young's generation, were something less than a novelty by then, something more than a lark.

Tonight's the Night, an album recorded in 1973 shortly after the drug overdose deaths of two of Young's friends (Danny Whitten, a member of Crazy Horse, and Bruce Berry, a tour assistant), was recorded one night as his band got high and played. Young has said that hallucinogens provide, for some artists, a means to creative expression; on the other hand, he counsels caution in their use, having witnessed the personal destruction that must follow addiction. For his own part, Young claimed in 1979 never to have taken LSD or heroin, although he freely admits to having smoked marijuana.

Young's record company, Reprise, tried to convince Young the album should not be released. But it was released, in 1975. In the liner notes to *Decade* (1979), he wrote, in reference to *Tonight's the Night*, "I think this is one of my strongest and longest lasting albums. It covers my obsession with the ups and downs of the drug culture." Young has also called the album "the darker side to *Harvest*."

The songs Young has written about drugs and the counterculture associated with them are quite different from the Beatles' contemplations of the subject, such as "Strawberry Fields Forever." "Out of My Mind" has a sense of "otherworldliness," a result mainly of Young's hypnotic and tired voice, the dragging rhythms of the guitar, and the haunting lyrics: "All I hear are screams from outside the limousine/ That are taking me out of my mind." Similarly, "Ambulance Blues," from *On the Beach* (1974), hints at the imagery and mood that *Tonight's the Night* was to introduce; indeed, the tracks would have been recorded at approximately the same time, since *Night* was withheld for a couple of years.

The Artistic Intuitions of a Solitary Man

That Young has worked both with and without a band provides further evidence that his prime concern has always been to find and challenge the limits of artistic accomplishment. By alternately seeking and forsaking the influences — but also the restrictions — of artistic collaboration, Young ensures that it is his own artistic intuitions that are the principal impetus for his creative life. The romantic, after all, is a solitary figure. It is clear that the choice of using a band, or not, is always his. The occasional desire to seek solitude as a creative mode is certainly part of the singer-songwriter's traditional stance. Perhaps, as well, Young follows the pattern that is characteristic of other Canadian popular musicians. Except for the supergroups the Guess Who (with its international hits "These Eyes" and "Laughing") and the Band (which gained enormous success with its collaboration with Bob Dylan), Canadians have tended to go it alone, in both writing and performing. The phenomenon is related to that other undefinable aspect of Canadian popular music — space — which manifests itself in the desire to gain the kind of distance that allows contemplation and reflection in the only way that is possible, through solitude.

In this regard, the inner and outer album jackets of *After the Gold Rush* are most compelling images of solitude and of solitary determination. In fact, the image of the cowboy, that most solitary of North American archetypes, appears throughout Young's work.

There is a well-known story of Young's journey to California in an old Pontiac hearse — a kind of latter-day covered wagon. Five others came along with him for the ride, but it was only Neil who knew where he was going, what he was looking for. The metaphor begs to be fashioned: in the days of the West's settlement, in Canada as in the US, many moved westward, but few had the resolve and foresight to stay, just as Young set out with others but succeeded on his own. Young has retained his aloneness — artistically and, by living far from the centres of production and culture, personally as well — in the face of tremendous pressure. That pressure is a result of not only his wealth, but also of the psychological prodding that a popular artist continually feels from his audience.

Co-existing with the motive of loneliness in Young's lyrics is that of death. "Thrasher," from *Rust Never Sleeps*, is thick with metaphors, many of them paired: the ancient river and the asphalt highway, the eagle and the vulture, the sun and the moon. The song evokes, in its apocalyptic references, the mood of "After the Gold Rush." It is a song about the sorrow and loss that are only hinted at in *Harvest*: "The motel of lost companions waits/ with heated pool and bar." The most memorable aspect of the song is the manner in which the simple strophic structure is continually undermined and put at risk by the relentless and daunting imagery: "They were lost in rock formations/ Or became park bench mutations." Romantic longing appears throughout Young's work; in "Thrasher" it reaches a level of unsurpassed balefulness.

The mood of Young's songs can be attributed in part to his often frail health. At the age of five, he contracted polio. After a long period of convalescence, he recovered and suffered no lasting effects. However, he has suffered from what he described as a "weak side," for which he has had to have surgery. Between the release of *After the Gold Rush* and that of *Harvest* he was in and out of hospital. He stated in a 1988 interview with *Musician* magazine that he began to work out three times a week, because he was "emaciated" to the point that he was having trouble even picking up his guitar. Young also suffers from epilepsy. In an interview with Cameron Crowe of *Rolling Stone*, Young talked about the experience of having an epileptic seizure: "Your body's flapping around and you're biting your tongue and batting your head on the ground but your mind is off somewhere else. The only scary thing about it is not going or being there, it's realizing you're totally comfortable in this ... *void*." He has also been reported to suffer from acidosis and diabetes.

For Young, these ailments seem to be, not debilities, but creative forces, as he told *Musician* magazine: "When I'm sick, when I have a temperature or feel ill, that's usually the most creative period for me." He claims to have written three of his best-known songs — "Down by the River," "Cowgirl in the Sand" and "Cinnamon Girl" — in one afternoon while ill, and to have recorded most of *Harvest* while wearing a brace.

Young's Old Ways

It is difficult to reconcile the image of Young dressed in his always-patched jeans and workshirt with the kind of opulence that his wealth could purchase. Indeed, early in his career, it must have seemed irreconcilable to Young himself. As his father relates, when Young visited London, England, in 1971, he refused to stay in the expensive flat in Grosvenor Square that had been provided for him. But if a wealthy man wants any privacy at all, he has to pay a great deal of money for it: when visiting the Canadian Rockies, Young has stayed in the Presidential Suite of the Banff Springs Hotel, which costs $3,000 per night. While he spends money on classic cars, a yacht and his sprawling ranch, he has been concerned with ensuring that he does not become enslaved by the trappings of rock. He has used his money to choose his creative projects carefully and to maintain meaningful contact with his audience and with his family. In 1976, for example, he played at small bars in northern California, lingering afterwards to talk to patrons. Often travelling in a bus rather than a jet, he visits his extended family when he can. He has thus escaped the personal and artistic decadence that has accompanied the success of other wealthy rockers. As a result, he has been able to continue to grow artistically.

In confirmation of Young's determination to maintain some kind of inner life, some kind of personal existence, Scott Young ends his book with a touching observation of the domestic life his son has chosen. As he told *Musician* magazine, Neil seemed touched by portions of his father's book: "I learned a lot about myself that I didn't know, because I saw myself through his eyes. And that was a real learning experience — to see myself as a kid now that I'm a parent." Young attributes his temporary "conversion" to country music, as evidenced by the release of *Old Ways* in 1985, to the essentially familial nature of country music, as he told *Musician* magazine: "I felt country music was really a family thing. It represented family values in a lot of ways, and real-life stories of families. That's why I related strongly to it, and I still do." An indication of Young's determination in this regard is his decision to spend most of a couple of years helping to provide intensive therapy to his son Ben — one of Young's two sons, both of whom suffer from cerebral palsy. In 1989, an album of songs by artists such as Nick Cave and others, singing songs by Young, was released, the proceeds from which would go to a school for children with cerebral palsy called the Bridge in Hillsborough, California. Young, too, has performed in aid of the school.

Young's desire to uphold family values cannot account entirely for his interest in country music and particularly for his release of *Old Ways*. He has often been asked about the album. In response to such a question at the end of an interview with rock journalist Bill Flanagan, Young tried to suggest a conceptual map of rock, country and the blues. With Flanagan he put together a compelling explanation: while country and blues form an arc of emotional and artistic impulses — with country represented by the initial ascending half of the half-circle and blues by the descent — rock finds no return to the baseline. Instead, it soars continuously upward. As such, rock must claim its fatalities, requiring as it does a kind of demonic energy to sustain. Country music — and blues, too, as the release of *This Note's for You* has confirmed — provides a musical release for Young, one which does not demand the torch-like intensity of rock but which still allows him to explore the poetic motives of his previous work. Young is not the only rock survivor to have found such a refuge. Van Morrison has retreated occasionally — but with intensity, as his recording with the Chieftains shows — to Irish folk song. For Young, such a retreat is the only sign that he must occasionally refrain from moving on. Country music is for him a single step back that inevitably precedes three steps forward.

Audiences reacted with disappointment to Young's stylistic departures in *Old Ways*. But this was not the only album to have enraged or disenchanted Young's audiences: *Journey Through the Past*, *Hawks & Doves*, *Trans* and *Landing on Water* have all had a similar effect. Yet Young's solitary artistic stance is no marketing gimmick, or merely a pose for his album covers. Remember, it was Young, not the other passengers in the hearse bound for California, who was determined to reach the promised land, no matter the cost. Young has repeatedly challenged the economic exigencies of the rocker's relationship to the music industry.

Confrontation and Control
in the Music Industry

To consider the most recent episode of Young's confrontation with the popular music industry, his challenge to the commercial sponsors of rock videos and concerts, it is important first to understand Young's long-standing interest in film. Here again, his efforts have been intense and sustained. He recorded the soundtrack for the autobiographical *Journey Through the Past* (1972). *Rust Never Sleeps* (1979), which Young directed and edited under the pseudonym of Bernard Shakey, is a documentary of himself in concert. In addition, Young has worked on several currently unfinished projects: he filmed his 1987 tour of Europe, which he says he intends to develop into a film, and he worked on a project called *Human Highway*. Finally, with the release of *Freedom*, Young produced a live performance that aired on Superchannel in January 1990.

Young's video for "Rockin' in the Free World" from *Freedom* (1989) appeared a few months earlier. As with many other rock videos, this one includes parallel narratives, one of a performance of the song — in this case, Young playing "live" with a band — and another of something to illustrate some of the ideas in the song, in this case Young as a "bag lady," wandering the streets of a city, pushing a shopping cart. The video includes many references to contemporary political and social motifs: "thousand points of light," George Bush's presidential campaign slogan, flashes across a screen; the "statue of liberty" erected during the 1989 Chinese student uprising crashes to the ground; cocaine is consumed. The song illustrates one of the ideas Young has stated in interviews in recent years: that there is something mortally wrong with American society, that perhaps the experiment in virtually unfettered individual freedom has brought with it deep-seated and permanent evils. This is made vivid aurally at the end of "On Broadway," when Young screams, with disturbing passion, "Gimme that crack!"

In spite of his interest in film and his production of videos, he says he has reservations about videos, especially regarding their increasing use as sales vehicles. The title cut from *This*

Note's for You (1988) became newsworthy when the sponsors of MTV (the US rock music cable channel) tried to have the video of the song banned from broadcast. It is easy to see why, after listening to the first few moments of the song, during which Young sings the following lines: "Ain't singing for Pepsi/ Ain't singing for Coke/ I don't sing for nobody/ Makes me look like a joke." Lawsuits were threatened; Young called MTV executives "spineless twerps." In the end the song was banned, on the grounds that MTV's policy prohibited the repeated use of brand names in a video. Still, the song — along with the album and Young himself — received more publicity than usually accompanies a Young release.

For Young, the controversy over "This Note's for You" struck directly at his philosophy of art. Music for him is a means of emotional communication, a direct line that is set up between him and his audience. To use that line for an ulterior purpose, such as selling beer or running shoes, is, to Young's mind, to corrupt it utterly. The situation with MTV also touched on Young's conviction that his artistic line of communication must not be hindered by a third party. Young started as a self-described folksinger and has maintained his commitment to communicating directly with "the people." In a dispute he had with Geffen records over the lack of commercial appeal of *Old Ways*, he said, at one point, that if the record company was, as it stated, interested only in producing what the "public" wanted, then it should go directly to that public and solicit its opinion. Young's views are connected to the way he records his songs, which he tries to keep as simple and direct as possible.

Many of Young's recorded songs sound as if they were released after the first take, which in many cases they were. While Young takes a large measure of control over the recording process, including mixing and mastering — which he does at his own studio on his ranch in San Mateo County in California — if the first try at a song yields the result he wants, he doesn't try to improve it. "Will to Love," for example, was recorded in a single evening. Young says he tries as much as possible to avoid consciously "editing" as he writes a song. "The thing is not to stop," he told *Musician* in 1988. "People don't want to hear what I think a cool song is. They want to hear a song that I wrote." Young tries to see that nothing, not even fussy "retakes" and editing, comes between him and his audience.

In the MTV dispute, on the other hand, there was no doubt that something had come between him and the audience he writes for. He has said that he sees videos — commercialized or not — as detracting from the "depth" of pure music. His doubts about the validity of *any* video as an artistic vehicle for music must only have compounded his frustration at the commotion over his own. To have gone to the effort, expense and trouble of producing a video, only to have it banned, must have seemed ironic.

In Young's early songs, the themes are the frontier, the ironic loneliness of the lover, the victim. The limousine (the poetic manifestation of his hearses), the American Indian, and the needle are at the core of his imagery. But his recent albums, aside from *Freedom*, are more difficult to digest. Rather than seeking unity through the choice of a few images and themes, Young allows a musical style or a single idea to become the arbiter for his musical expression. (Each album, then, is like an aesthetic hairpin turn in a mountain road. It's hard to know where it's taken you until you've come out of it and see the next one coming.) This method of bringing material together for an album began in earnest with the release of *Hawks & Doves*. It found its most bizarre and unappealing expression in *Trans* and *Everybody's Rockin'*. No one wants to listen to an album with the vocals on six of the nine tracks fed through a digital something-or-other; similarly, twenty-four minutes of rockabilly, no matter how venerable the singer, doesn't quite cut it.

Young has strolled down most of popular music's alleyways: rock (with homages to punkers and rock-and-rollers alike), folk, country and pop (including techno-pop experiments). It's an amorphous *oeuvre*. Trying to discern a direction is difficult, although listening to *Decade*, Young's 1977 retrospective, at least provides an overview of the music's scope. Howard Hampton of *Village Voice* has unkindly attributed the diversity and volume of Young's output to Young's function as a "cultural garbage can." A writer for the *Globe and Mail* tried to personalize the phenomenon by comparing Young to a crazy old uncle, the man you love but don't always understand, the one who you can count on to say odd things to your friends.

The Romantic Hero

Decade, a three-album compilation of Young's best songs which was released in 1977, remains a powerful statement of Young's achievement up to that point. More significantly, *Decade* is a signpost that points to his later albums, with their concentration on common concerns: the rise of technology in society, the spiritual danger of wealth and the continuous search for love. The album contains Young's hits alongside his most artistically ambitious efforts. Thus, "Heart of Gold," Young's most popular single is included, as is his long and moving "Cortez the Killer." *Decade* offers the listener the advantage of avoiding the distractions of some of Young's less successful work. Thus, for example, although Young considers *Tonight's the Night* to be his most significant album, *Decade* contains only a couple of cuts from it: the title song (part one) and "Tired Eyes." The collection contains a definable set of images and themes: estranged love, solitude, the frontier, and oppressor and victim. And they *are* themes, not simply idea tags repeated occasionally, for Young treats each idea with literary care and objectivity. For the theme of oppressor and victim, for example, we hear an indictment of Richard Nixon as oppressor (in "Ohio") and then a reflection on his fate as victim (in "Campaigner"). *Decade* will not be Young's last retrospective: he is working on a twenty-fifth anniversary collection that will apparently feature the best of his career, along with some previously unreleased tracks.

I suppose that for a songwriter whose lyrics are essentially romantic, it is most appropriate for me to reach for a romantic image to account for Neil Young's appeal. In Young there is the quality of the childlike hero: according to various accounts, as a child he was victimized by schoolyard bullies, but he fought back with energy and determination. Similarly, after countless experiences that might have weathered the heart and rendered Young the kind of hard-shelled "personality" that rock's most famous practitioners seem to be, he, on the other hand, finds the affection and sentiment within himself to call his father "daddy." In my most fervid contemplation of all of this, I see Neil Young in the embrace of that "cosmic void" of the seizures he himself has described. Gripping the guitar's neck, whose yaw he both controls and is controlled by, he sings, the childlike, flat-timbred voice soaring upward and outward — for a glorious moment holding back the darkness. As he grows old.

Neil Young — The Best

Song: "Old Man"

Album: *After the Gold Rush*

Article for further reading: Bill Flanagan, "The Real Neil Young Stands Up," *Musician* no. 85 (November 1985): 32-36+

Discography

Neil Young (1968)
Everybody Knows This Is Nowhere (1969)
After the Gold Rush (1970)
Harvest (1972)
Journey Through the Past [film soundtrack] (1972)
Time Fades Away [live] (1973)
On the Beach (1974)
Tonight's the Night (1975)
Zuma (1975)
Long May You Run (1976)
American Stars 'N Bars (1977)
Decade [compilation] (1977)
Comes a Time (1978)
Rust Never Sleeps (1979)
Live Rust [live] (1979)
Hawks & Doves (1980)
Re-ac-tor (1981)
Trans (1982)
Everybody's Rockin' (1983)
Old Ways (1985)
Landing on Water (1986)
Life (1987)
This Note's for You (1988)
Freedom (1989)

Harvest moon (1991)
unpluged (1993)

4·Our Lady of the Canyon: Joni Mitchell

It's just that some steps outside the Boho dance
Have a fascination for me
— "The Boho Dance"

On one bitterly cold night during my childhood in Edmonton, under a sky black and perfectly clear, I was playing "pom-pom pull-away" with a hundred other kids at the local outdoor skating rink. The rink was nestled in a bowl created by a hill surrounding it on two sides, so the whoops of the other kids echoed and were quickly hushed in the surrounding boards. The experience was much like it is and has always been for any other Canadian child. However, at a certain point in the evening, I became aware of the fierce beauty of it all: the cold, the absolute clarity and stillness of the air, the phosphorescent blue lights and the colourful surge of bodies across the creaking ice. The answer to the question of *who I was* seemed startlingly clear that night: I was one of the others who experienced the same sensations of a cold Canadian night that I did. Everyone playing the game — neighbour, friend, sibling — was linked to the other by the particular experience of hearing the dry squeak of skate blades on ice and of sensing bodily the headlong push to reach the other side of the rink. Perhaps the act of skating is as prototypically Canadian as any other physical action. Jane Siberry has written about it in her song "Hockey"; Joni Mitchell in "River."

"River," which appears on Mitchell's masterpiece album, *Blue*, is a good illustration of the paradoxes of Mitchell's career. In the lyrics of the song, a frozen river seemed to provide for

Mitchell the image of a route to comfort and release: "Oh I wish I had a river/ I could skate away on/ I made my baby cry." Yet at the time she recorded "River," Mitchell was living in California, not Saskatchewan. Mitchell's childhood and adolescence in Canada have been important influences in the refinement of her sensibilities as a poet and composer. That she is considered, and considers herself, a composer of "American music" is another of the delicious paradoxes that have marked Mitchell's life and career, and there are more: she seeks to reconcile artistic achievement with popular success; she has chosen a public venue for expressing very private concerns; she is painter and poet, composer and producer; she is an innocent possessed of wealth.

Roberta Joan Anderson was born in Fort Macleod, Alberta, on Nov. 7, 1943. She grew up in Saskatoon and studied art at Alberta College in Calgary. Still a teenager, she moved to Toronto where she began her career as a folksinger. She moved to the US in 1966 where she married Chuck Mitchell, a Detroit folksinger, from whom she was later divorced. Mitchell's career was started with the assistance of ex-Byrd David Crosby, who produced her first album, *Song to a Seagull*, and singer Judy Collins, who recorded Mitchell's "Both Sides Now" when Mitchell was still relatively unknown.

Aside from an aborted attempt in the 1970s to live in the Canadian bush, she has continued to live in the US, although she maintains a residence in Vancouver. In 1976, *Stereo Review* writer Noel Coppage wrote an illuminating article in which he illustrated the geographical and spiritual contrasts between Mitchell's childhood home in Saskatoon and her chosen home, Los Angeles. In Saskatoon, the eye might search in vain for geographical relief; Los Angeles, on the other hand, is a canyon. In Mitchell's first home, temperance and respect for authority were strictly observed; in the second, all rules were thrown out.

The events in the childhood, adolescence and young adulthood of Joni Mitchell have much in common with those of Neil Young: a fight against polio as a child, failure at school, beginnings as a folksinger at the Riverboat Folk Club in Toronto, ambivalence to an adopted homeland and a tireless effort to resist the pressures of the popular music industry. With regard to the latter, *The Hissing of Summer Lawns* (1975) was to Joni

Mitchell what *Tonight's the Night* was to Neil Young. Both albums allowed their creators to satisfy a long-felt need to try to change an industry that they felt was hampering their creative spirits. For *Hissing*, the method for asserting a creative identity was Mitchell's refusal to include the kind of tunes associated with accessible popular music; for *Tonight*, it was Young's decision to present an unflinching chronicle of a descent into the psychic abyss of drug addiction. But both musicians felt the sting of their decision: *Rolling Stone* called Mitchell's album the worst of the year, and Young's popularity, measured by record sales, has never returned to previous levels.

Seeking Dualities in Art

Even though she has created a remarkable body of work over the years, Joni Mitchell still has not found the kind of respect that other musicians — especially those in the jazz and high art genres — have experienced early in their careers. In 1978, Don Heckman of *High Fidelity* magazine wrote: "If snobbism toward pop music was not still rampant in the halls of academe, I'm sure Mitchell would be rightfully acknowledged as one of the most significant creative musical talents of this generation." She is careful to shun the élitism of high art, stating that her music — and her painting, for that matter — is for a large audience.

Still, Mitchell is intensely aware of the tension between popular and high art. It is perhaps the most public of the paradoxes at the heart of her creative life. For example, while she has called her creations "art songs," her musical lineage is through the English folk tradition, which is characterized by the careful setting of words to refined melodies and by an emphasis on the formal structure of a song. In common with other popular musicians who have their roots in the folk idiom, she seeks in her music "naturalness" and "honesty," measuring her songs' success by these criteria.

But all *successful* folksingers eventually reach a point of commercial and artistic success where they must choose one of three paths. They may maintain their conception of "natural" singing, in which case their audience is likely to stay the same or shrink, as listeners themselves change their tastes. Or, in the interests of increased fame and wealth, they may decide to abandon their commitment to integral human expression through art and simply try to sell records by writing to formula. Finally — and this is the path Mitchell took — they may try to remain close to the impulse to create, while loosening their grip on the *means* of creation. Mitchell has expanded her means of musical creation to include the jazz and rock idioms and any number of musical instruments, including such "unnatural" ones as synthesizers. Indeed, "Smokin' " features the rhythmic clunking of a cigarette machine as the basis of the percussion track.

As for how to measure such characteristics as naturalness or honesty, perhaps the best we can do is to suggest that the closer that folk music stays to the unaffected impulse to express, the more "natural" it is. This seems to be the way Mitchell regards her work. According to her, *Blue* is her best, because it reveals her emotions nakedly. *Clouds* is not as good, since she was, at the time, influenced by the vocal style of Crosby, Stills, Nash and Young. To Mitchell, then, a great artist is a fully developed *individual*.

What is her artistic goal? "I'm looking to make modern American music," she said in an interview in *Rolling Stone*. Mitchell's music possesses the sophistication of jazz, the directness and honesty of rock, and the "natural" sounds and sensibilities of folk. The respected *Musician* magazine featured as one of its cover stories in 1988 four "living legends" of American music. Subtitled "Four Corners of American Music," the four legends included Stevie Wonder, Sonny Rollins, Johnny Cash and Mitchell. Mitchell has practically created her own genre, although it doesn't have a name — that of the eclectic whose influences can be assimilated in the idiom of popular music while possessing the coherence and unity of a body of music that any "high art" composer would envy. But she has also said, as quoted in *Time*: "It was then and still is a constant war to liberate myself from values not applicable to the period in which I live." To these ends, she takes as much control over the entire creative process as she can.

But the ultimate criterion of a popular artist's work — and this is borrowed from the realm of high art —is its staying power, its ability to sustain interest many years after its creation. In this respect, some of Mitchell's songs ("Both Sides Now," "The Circle Game") still bear listening, even after a couple of decades. To date, *Blue* is the album that has displayed the most artistic resilience. Commercially, it has sold 1.3 million copies in the US alone. Released in 1971, it is still commercially available today. It is the most striking example of Mitchell's ability to wed two seemingly contradictory values: artistic achievement and commercial success.

Blue is spare and simple in its arrangements, melodies and lyrical structures. The most distinctive musical aspect of the album is James Taylor's dulcimer-like guitar playing on the opening cuts on each side, "All I Want" and "California." The muted and poignant sound of these songs provides the cue for the unified mood of the album. Similarly, the piano accompaniment on "My Old Man" is played by Mitchell sensitively and without artifice; there are two verses followed by a bridge, another verse and bridge, and a repeat of the first verse. The verses express a motive treated often in popular music, the expression of affection for a lover; the bridge describes the "blue" times when the lover is absent. The song's structure is as simple as it is possible to make it. But there are resonances. The tentativeness of the lovers' bond is suggested each time the singer states that she and her lover "don't need no piece of paper/ from the city hall/ keeping us tied and true" and each time the bridge describes the nights the singer spends alone. The intimacy of the song is reinforced each time a reference is made to the metaphor of music: the lover is "the warmest chord I ever heard" and a "singer in the park."

The musical motives on *Blue* serve to enclose the emotional territory of the songs. Its musical unity is accomplished through the use of a limited number of instruments, usually used singly in the accompaniment. Mitchell's solo voice, while exploring various registers, assumes the same quality of warmth and calm throughout. The lyrics are deceptively simple, as the example from "My Old Man" illustrates. They successfully make the leap from the specific (and these are very specific songs about very specific people and situations) to the universal. The feeling of insularity on the album is almost tangible. Interestingly, Henry Lewy, the engineer, has said that this is physically how the album was recorded: during the studio sessions the door was locked, barring anyone but those involved in the sessions from entering.

The intensely personal references on *Blue* are all the more striking for the fact that the songs have found such wide appeal. But Mitchell's song-writing is characterized by paradoxes similar to this one. Ariel Swartley of *Rolling Stone* has described the ironies and ambiguities of Mitchell's song-writing by suggesting she has a dual persona: that of siren and that of symbolist. The role of siren is to be heard on albums such as *Court and Spark* and *Hejira*; that of symbolist is to be heard on *For the Roses* and *The Hissing of Summer Lawns*.

Mitchell has consistently used a very public art form, her songs, as an expression of very private feelings, those related to her spiritual journey. Prominent in her diary of songs are the stories of her love relationships. She is reported to have had romantic relationships with Stephen Stills, Graham Nash, Neil Young, Leonard Cohen and Jackson Browne. Of course, attention to her love life is unfair: no one keeps track of the amorous efforts of male singers. Certainly, Mitchell has been a seeker in her personal life. Stephen Holden of *Rolling Stone* has said: "Perhaps more directly than anyone except Mick Jagger, Joni Mitchell has always acknowledged the inseparability of sexual curiosity and rock music. Having satisfied her curiosity, Mitchell probably knows better than most of us the high price to be paid for such knowledge." Mitchell says that it took her until age forty to find a mate and that now she can turn her attention to other things. She is married to Larry Klein, a bass player, who now co-produces Mitchell's albums with her. She has no children.

Mitchell's folk influence has had an effect throughout her career, but she has often foiled that influence by pursuing other musical idioms. For example, as a result of her concern with the art of bending, stretching and splicing the melodic line — the primary activity of the folk songwriter — she found herself in the 1970s experimenting with her own style of an undulating jazz melodic line. This was first evident on *For the Roses* in 1972 and culminated with *Mingus* in 1979. The inspiration for *Mingus*, jazz bassist Charles Mingus himself, brought Mitchell close to the blues tradition which led to a foray, for the first time, into rock on the album *Wild Things Run Fast*.

Mitchell's background in jazz was limited at the time she began to record *Mingus*; furthermore, Mingus had been known as a musician hard to work with and was in fact consistently critical of whites. The question arises as to why Mingus chose to work with Mitchell, given the differences in their musical and personal backgrounds. But in fact, their ideas about music were quite similar. Both had a universal view of what constitutes music. They both valued all musical genres and felt that the sounds of nature — indeed of any environment — should be considered part of the composer's palette. Still, that Mitchell decided to work with an older black jazz musician follows her pattern of seeking dualities. A compelling visual depiction of this pattern can be seen on the cover of *Don Juan's Reckless Daughter* (1977), which features a photograph of Mitchell disguised as a black man.

The Critical "I"

Mitchell shares with countless folksingers the experience of recalling a point when she realized that poetry could be sung, that the love of metre and imagery could be transformed through the use of music. For Mitchell this revelation came about as she listened to the songs of Bob Dylan. Still, it makes only as much sense to say that Mitchell is a poet who deals in music than it is to say that Henry Moore was a painter who dealt in three dimensions. Such a separation of form and substance does nothing to illuminate an artist's work. What of the *dramatic* aspect of the composition, of that part of the song's essence that must be *heard* to be understood? Author Tom Manoff takes a refreshing and wholistic approach not only to Mitchell's music but to all music, popular or serious. Citing classical Greek theatre as an example, Manoff describes the *ancient unity* as an interplay of music (or song), dance and drama. He points out that dance, or motion, cannot be divorced from music, nor drama from song. Furthermore, he states, "poetry, as we know it, is a relatively late offspring of song. Song is the mother art." Mitchell is the personification of a conception of art that simply follows the human impulse to express experience or feeling through movement, gesture and sound. Her hesitancy to stifle or affect this impulse is the source of her retreats from public discourse and of her sensitivity to criticism.

Besides music, two important modes of expression for Mitchell are painting and movement. Some of her album covers — including, most notably, *Court and Spark* and *Mingus*

— feature her own paintings. Interestingly, she often tries to answer questions about her music with analogies from painting — as if music is for her an expression of something visual. As for movement, the inside cover of *Hejira* showing Mitchell skating is revealing, as are the album covers that feature her paintings, which often portray motion. In an interview published in *Rolling Stone*, she described her love of movement and dance this way: "I'll be standing in the kitchen and all of a sudden my body wants to jump around. For no reason at all. You've seen kids that suddenly just get a burst of energy? That part of my child is still alive." Similarly, she tells a story of attending a party where the guests were reluctant to dance. In frustration, she finally asked another woman to dance with her. In Mitchell's music, typical variations of the motive of movement are floating, skating and dancing. In "Amelia," the variation of flying is used to transcend all of these.

If Mitchell is aware of the tension between popular music and high art, she has been subject to the problems it creates for listeners and for critics. The ambiguity in this regard is evident in the critical literature surrounding popular music. This literature consists of periodicals for three audiences. First, there are the magazines and papers for fans or serious listeners. These include *Rolling Stone*, *Village Voice* and, in Great Britain, *Melody Maker*. While these began as "alternative" publications, they may now be more properly considered "lifestyle" magazines, since they portray popular music as simply one part of a singularly urban, affluent mode of existence. Also feeding the curiosity of fans are local newspapers and national newsmagazines, which often feature concert and record reviews as well as profiles of musicians. Second, there are the magazines for professional musicians, such as *Downbeat* and *Musician*. Third, there are the periodicals aimed at the music or entertainment industry. This group of publications includes *Billboard*, *Variety* and the like.

Each of these publications has a particular style of presenting the music and life of musicians. But common to many of them, especially those in the first category, is an analysis of popular songs as poetry. Here, the critical review takes the form of a search for themes and images in the lyrics. This approach calls for an examination of the songwriter's lyrical sensibilities. Of course, some of the trade and professional papers emphasize the business side of the musician's efforts (including, for example, comprehensive reports of the gross earnings of particular concerts) or even the technical aspects of choosing and playing the instruments. However, for those articles that attempt to provide some sort of critical framework for the creative output of a popular musician, the chosen mode of criticism is literary analysis of the lyrics.

This approach to the criticism of popular music has been only partly successful in providing an explication of what Joni Mitchell does. For while Mitchell's songs are consciously lyrical, the words do not always survive the leap to the printed page. But Mitchell writes songs to be heard, not poems to be read. They are part of a new oral tradition that has been established by popular music as it has developed in conjunction with the rise of recording technology. Through the medium of recorded sound, songwriters are now able to compose and perform their works exactly as they intend them. The words need not be considered separately from the "authoritative" version created by the composer. Furthermore, listeners have the opportunity to consult the recorded versions of the work of many other musicians, whether from the same genre or not. This has served to undermine the notion of poetry as written word and revive the notion of poetry as spoken or sung word.

However, the complicating factor in all of this is the commercial pressure to conform to the strait-jacket of popular music. To assure sales of her albums, Mitchell, like other popular musicians, has had to try to get a single played on the radio. But program managers have a rigid schedule of recordings, dictated partly by the need for advertising time slots and partly by the need to keep the "sound" of the station consistent and upbeat. It is almost impossible to get air-play for a song that is longer than the prescribed three or four minutes or that sounds too much *unlike* the other songs on the play-list, whether because of unusual instrumentation, reflective lyrics or a turgid tempo or rhythmic structure. Mitchell has often found it difficult to reconcile the contradictions of the pursuit of popular success and the aspiration to artistic accomplishment. If a musician, no matter how well known, tries to move beyond radio's strictures of commercial popular music, he or she is, in effect, censored. Because of this, it is difficult to find a mode of criticism entirely suited to the new art. Joni Mitchell has learned this to her distress.

The Hissing of Summer Lawns, which was almost universally panned by critics, illustrates some of the problems inherent in the dislocation of criticism and popular music. The album must, by any definition, be considered one of popular music. After all, Mitchell is, if nothing else, an artist for the people. Yet here Mitchell released something that was not easily digested by a mass audience. First, it was mainly jazz, an idiom that, for all its black grassroots beginnings, is an élite art form, played and listened to mainly by educated members of the middle class. There were few of the pop anchors on the album that allow accessibility: musical and lyrical hooks, memorable melodies or phrases. Second, the lyrics of the songs were difficult and "arty." None of this would necessarily make for a *bad* album, but it did stretch to the limit the genre that the album was cast in, that of popular music.

How to deal with this as a critic? Stephen Holden of *Rolling Stone* turned to the methods of literary criticism. Examining "Don't Interrupt the Sorrow," for example, he wrote, "The song parallels modern forms of female subjugation with both Christian and African mythology in imagery that is disjunctive and telegraphic." He went on to make similarly perceptive but, for the general listener — or, more to the point, record buyer — overly erudite, observations about the literary nuggets to be found on the album. In short, he discussed the success of the lyrics as literature. As it happened, he found the lyrics to be very *good* literature. Then, however, he stated the startling irony of all his gleanings: "If *The Hissing of Summer Lawns* offers substantial literature, it is set to insubstantial music." For all the sophistication of Mitchell's imagery, Holden found the album wanting — quite rightly — because his search for a "catchy tune" was largely unsuccessful.

At the end of his piece, Holden suggested that Mitchell should have worked with other musicians of "her own stature," such as the pop-jazz pianist Keith Jarrett. But the ambiguities at the heart of *The Hissing of Summer Lawns* were connected with matters more basic than those of personnel and personality. Mitchell stretched the pop genre further than it would go, and the arbiters of popular taste, who are much more rigid in their standards than one might assume, called her to account. For her part, Mitchell has commented on the nature of popular music standards, saying that a pop artist is criticized as bitterly for being "too commercial" as for being "inaccessible."

As a collection of avant-garde pop, the album is full of delights. It is one of my favourites. The reason for the album's failure in the eyes of the critics — and, for that matter, its failure to sell well — is the high proportion of experimental pieces. Ironically, this is the type of song that has helped Mitchell develop her style. "The Jungle Line" features mainly Mitchell's voice and guitar, a synthesizer playing a simple bass line with upper register imitations, and African drums. Similarly, "Shadows and Light" has a severe electronic accompaniment (played by an instrument called an Arp-Farfisa). Neither song is a candidate for the top forty. "Harry's House — Centerpiece" features the interpolation of a well-known song by Johnny Mandel and Jon Hendricks, written in 1958. The album's melody lines are typically amorphous and indistinguishable, but they are mesmerizing — an appropriate effect, given the album's themes. Even on "Edith and the Kingpin," a song whose lyrics speak of the enslavement of hooker by pimp, the melody simply floats along.

The album's evocative title is keyed to Mitchell's own cover illustration, a remarkable landscape, executed in muted tones of silver-grey and green, featuring what I take to be a depiction of some tribal rite in the foreground and an urban skyline in the background. But the inside photo, which shows Mitchell floating, suspended in a pool, perhaps her own, provides the artistic cue for the music. This is music in suspended motion; it is finding its own path. The image of floating is a significant one in Mitchell's music. There are lines throughout *Don Juan's Reckless Daughter* that refer to this sensation. On a personal level, Mitchell has said that her swimming pool is one luxury she doesn't question. Here are some lines from "Black Crow" (on *Hejira*): "In search of love and music/ My whole life has been/ Illumination/ Corruption/ And diving, diving, diving, diving."

The lyrics, the musical style, the album cover — all contribute to the unity of this work. Perhaps it is *too* unified. Perhaps that is what made it such a commercial flop. In any case, what Mitchell did that could not be forgiven by the critics was to create something that pushed the limits of popular music too far and too fast. That the audience and critics of pop are much less tolerant of experimentation than are those of other musical genres is an irony that has not escaped Mitchell. The struggle to grow artistically has been, it seems, personally painful, as she stated in a *Rolling Stone* interview: "You can stay the same and protect the formula that gave you your initial success. They're going to crucify you for staying the same. If you change, they're going to crucify you for changing.... I'd rather be crucified for changing." However, Mitchell seems to underestimate the goodwill that her listeners feel for her, preferring to give undue credence to the views of professional critics. She has expressed bitterness about the negative reviews she has received of such albums as *The Hissing of Summer Lawns* and *Don Juan's Reckless Daughter*.

On the other hand, *Shadows and Light*, unlike Mitchell's other live album (*Miles of Aisles*), received the endorsement of virtually all reviewers. The choice of songs for the album is part of the reason: aside from "Woodstock," the album was a selection of her most evocative compositions. Recorded five years after *The Hissing of Summer Lawns*, the album is, in a way, a confirmation of Mitchell's explorations on the earlier album — regardless of the critical backlash *Hissing* received — since it includes three of the ten tracks from *Hissing*. Another reason the album was so successful is the quality of Mitchell's band, which was a grouping of jazz's most popular and talented musicians: Pat Metheny (guitar), Jaco Pastorius (bass guitar), Don Alias (drums and percussion), Lyle Mays (keyboards), Michael Brecker (saxophone) and the Persuasions (vocals).

Shadows and Light also features a haunting and very beautiful performance of "Amelia," first recorded on *Hejira*. Mitchell's voice is calm and tender as she sings about looking up into the sky and imagining six jet streams as the strings on her guitar. This is a wispy song, suggesting the experience of flight in both the lilting rhythms and the repetitive structure (there are seven verses). The metaphor of flight is reinforced as the sound of airplane engines is compared to that of a song. And then, in one of the most beautiful moments in the tradition of confessional song-writing, the metaphor of flight is pulled down to earth to confront earthly concerns: "Maybe I've never really loved/ I guess that is the truth/ I've spent my whole life in clouds at icy altitudes." Singing live, Mitchell achieves the vulnerability the song requires through extending the melodic line beyond the song's formal structure. Her caressing of the name "Amelia" is among Mitchell's most tender effects. Pat Metheny's electric guitar, which begins on the fifth verse, extends a solo after the end of the song into a musical depiction of flight.

Charting an Artistic Flight Path

Mitchell's earliest albums helped create for her an artistic persona of innocence. But if Mitchell is an innocent, she has still had to deal with her wealth and some of the ugly things that go with it. Litigation, burglaries and the petty envies of other musicians: these have encroached on Mitchell's ability to continue to maintain the attitude of the innocent. Critic Bart Testa has observed that "her problems are the problems of a middle-class woman of means." She acknowledged as much in an interview in *Musician* magazine: "Now I have to grow teeth and protect [my money]. I have to grow a kind of wildness that I don't really want, because I don't want to endanger my innocence." This has created a paradoxical situation in which she finds she must criticize the very sources of her power. Yet the contradiction of this imperative is not considered in her lyrics. As a result, there is a bleak irony to some of her songs. Examples can be found on *Dog Eat Dog*, released in 1985, in which she sings about the evils of materialism.

Thus, with the release of *Dog Eat Dog*, Mitchell turned her focus from relations of love to those of the social contract. She refers to two types of victimization in the lyrics of the album. The first is a result of geo-political disparities dealt with in "Ethiopia"; the second is the economic cannibalism of which Mitchell feels she herself is a victim. Mitchell sensed a tangible increase in greed in North America in the 1980s. She was burglarized, sued by her housekeeper, and over-taxed by the State of California. She responded to the latter by suing the State in 1983, an action she won in 1988. The motive of victim and prey is found in each song on *Dog Eat Dog*, even in "Smokin'," a very short, whimsical song about the mutual dependence of smoker and cigarette manufacturer. Mitchell deals directly with the particulars of politics ("Ethiopia"), religion ("Tax Free"), and society ("Shiny Toys"). Outside of her musical life, her efforts to highlight social ills led her, in May 1989, to participate in the recording of a song entitled "The Spirit of the Forest," a single whose proceeds would go to fight the deforestation of tropical rain forests. In 1984 she had helped record the single "Tears Are Not Enough," which was produced and sold to provide relief to famine victims in Ethiopia.

In addition to her reputation as songwriter and performer, Mitchell is known as a highly skilled producer; along with her husband, she maintains strong control over the recording process. Her skills in the recording studio began to have demonstrable effect in 1973, with the release of the masterfully produced and mixed *Court and Spark*. Traditionally, the composer used the manuscript (the printed form of the music) to provide a permanent record of his or her musical intentions. However, recording has become an important part of the act of composition, because today the recorded version of a piece of music is often the authoritative version — even, increasingly, in the realm of high art music. Mitchell has become skilled at directing, recording, editing and mixing, because she realizes these, too, are now the skills of the composer.

As a composer of popular music, Mitchell does what the high art composer does and has always done: fashion musical ideas while providing an authoritative source that indicates the "intentions" of the composer in as detailed a form as possible. The *means* by which Mitchell composes is likewise identical to that of a high art composer. It comes down to two main activities: experimenting with and extending previously developed musical forms, and drawing on other musical sources. That Mitchell has a well-defined audience that she must keep in mind as she composes puts her in such revered company as Haydn and Handel. These composers had to work within certain formal restrictions; to have done otherwise would have resulted in the censure of their work and financial and personal ruin. Whether it is a fickle opera audience or the kid who has come into a store to buy a record makes no difference: the bottom line is that certain stylistic expectations have always restricted the work of the composer.

In mastering the art of recording and spending less time performing in public (she has not gone on a major tour since 1979), Mitchell is following the lead of other musicians, the most famous of which were the Beatles, who abandoned touring after only a few years to devote their time to recording. In disappointment, many fans attributed this move to the cynicism and arrogance that wealth can bring to popular musicians. There is no doubt that some performers eventually decide that the personal and professional pressures of performing in public outweigh the benefits.

Chalk Mark in a Rainstorm is a showcase for Mitchell's skills as a composer and producer. The album features contributions by venerable popular musicians Peter Gabriel, Tom Petty, Billy Idol, Willie Nelson and Don Henley. It was put together using sophisticated recording technology. For example, "Dancin' Clown" was recorded as a kind of short film or drama, albeit using the medium of recorded sound only. The song portrays a bully named Rowdy Yates (whose lines are sung by Billy Idol) and a victim named Jesse ("played" by Tom Petty). In order to create the repartee of the two "actors," Mitchell used sampling (the capture in digital form of sounds which are then processed in various ways) and other technological tricks to get the effects she wanted. More than any other album, *Chalk Mark* displays Mitchell's skills as a modern composer.

Mitchell has taken control, not only of her artistic destiny, but also of her business affairs. Because her new albums are expensive to produce, she has been pressured to put out a "greatest hits" album. However, she has resisted this pressure, since such an album would dry up whatever sales are continuing of her earlier albums. It is a courageous decision and a sign that, like Neil Young — but very much *unlike* some of her colleagues — Mitchell takes a strong grip on her professional life. Even early in her career, she made do without a manager, booking tours and managing the money herself. Today, her involvement in her business affairs extends to personally checking requests to reprint her lyrics.

Her personal and professional courage is reflected in her lyrics. In all of Mitchell's explorations of the reaches of human emotion, despair never appears in her lyrics. As the lyrics from the title cut of *Blue* state, self-destruction is not the only road for the artist: "Well everybody's saying/ that hell's the hippest way to go/ Well I don't think so." Instead, in common with k.d. lang, Mitchell attributes magical qualities to some of her experiences. She seems to sense the hand of destiny in her work.

A couple of anecdotes illustrate this nicely. During the period she was trying to write lyrics to "Goodbye Pork Pie Hat" (a song written by Mingus in tribute to saxophonist Lester Young), Mitchell stepped off the subway to see a couple of black boys dancing on the street in front of a bar. The bar was called the Pork Pie Hat. The boys were dancing to jukebox music coming from inside the bar. There were posters of Young everywhere. Mitchell was able to finish her song. Another anecdote relates to Mitchell's relationship with Charles Mingus. Mingus died on Jan. 5, 1979, and his body was cremated the next day. The inside cover of *Mingus* states: "That same day fifty-six sperm whales beached themselves on the Mexican coastline and were removed by fire. These are the coincidences that thrill my imagination."

Magic, floating, flight, innocence: it takes courage to shelter the sensibilities from the forces that would corrupt such themes. Mitchell's voice remains the fresh, disorienting, beguiling influence it was when she began her career. Her voice still has that uncanny ability to follow the shifting directions of the melodies. She does not have a refined voice (even if she did, her heavy smoking habit would have roughened it by now), but she uses it like a virtuoso, shading the meaning of her poetic images and dramatizing the emotional peaks and valleys of the lyrics. If Neil Young's voice is used to edge out the rest of the universe, Joni Mitchell's voice is encompassing, inclusive. And while in the beginning it was the innocent voice alone that enchanted, today the authentic voice of the composer can be heard as well.

Joni Mitchell — The Best

Song: "Both Sides Now"

Album: *Blue*

Article for further reading: Bill Flanagan, "Joni Mitchell Loses Her Cool," *Musician* 86 (December 1985): 64-70+.

Discography

Song to a Seagull (1968)
Clouds (1969)
Ladies of the Canyon (1970)
Blue (1971)
For the Roses (1972)
Court and Spark (1974)
Miles of Aisles [live] (1974)
The Hissing of Summer Lawns (1975)
Hejira (1976)
Don Juan's Reckless Daughter (1977)
Mingus (1979)
Shadows and Light [live] (1980)
Wild Things Run Fast (1982)
Dog Eat Dog (1985)
Chalk Mark in a Rainstorm (1988)

5·Making Contact with Bruce Cockburn

Somewhere out there is a place that's cool
Where peace and balance are the rule.
— *"Waiting for a Miracle"*

In January of 1972, *Time* magazine named Richard Nixon their Man of the Year. In that same issue, Canadians as well as Americans were witnesses to war profiteering with a twist: smugglers were cutting open the bodies of slain American soldiers, stashing heroin in the corpses and sewing them up for shipment to the US. It was a grisly revelation that perhaps symbolized the social decay to which members of the counter-culture were pointing. For his part, Bruce Cockburn was writing the songs for *Sunwheel Dance*, an album whose lyrics, in the words of Katherine Gilday of the *Globe and Mail*, are filled with "stars and streams and blue space." Cockburn had retreated to a house in the country and was content to sing about the glories of domestic rural life.

The first song on *Sunwheel Dance* plays on the feudal titles "my lady and my Lord," referring not to a serf's masters, but to the poet's wife and God. This coyness was preventing Cockburn's music from becoming part of the Canadian mainstream.

Cockburn says that like many of his artistic colleagues, he was "reacting to the tenor of the times." But while they chose to use their art as a weapon against social decay, Cockburn's response was to withdraw, to set up contemplative distance between himself and the world.

The act of seeking solitude is one Cockburn has repeated throughout his career. As a songwriter concerned with the primacy of the written word, he seems to need to maintain a certain distance from the world. This is evident in the public events of Cockburn's life and in the lyrics of his songs. Distance has allowed him to rejuvenate his creative energies and to reflect on what he is becoming, personally and musically. This ability has been particularly important for Cockburn, since he has gone through distinct stages in his artistic and personal life. He has adopted, in turn, the personas of happy hermit, travelling troubadour, Christian ecstatic and, in the albums since *Dancing in the Dragon's Jaws*, social critic.

Members of his audience have been surprised, even dismayed, by each transformation. Cockburn's personality is complex; his demeanour is intense and fraught with the seriousness of life. But most fans have discerned Cockburn's integrity, and this has instilled loyalty. In fact, you will find that long-time fans of Bruce Cockburn (of which I'm one, of course) exhibit a certain fierce pride and perseverance; they're in it for the long haul and they aren't swayed much by their man's current idiosyncrasies. For my part, for example, I'm particularly attracted to Cockburn's "middle" period (albums such as *In the Falling Dark, Dancing in the Dragon's Jaws* and *Humans*), but I'll buy any album that Cockburn releases, even if the only tune on it is the sound of his refrigerator humming.

Yet a solitary poetic stance, the constant in Cockburn's career, is difficult for a popular musician to maintain. Myrna Kostash, who met and wrote about Cockburn in 1972, said later that most of Cockburn's contemporaries at the time were no longer living in the country: "The culture of that period was raw and dirty and mean and urban. I hated this throwback to rural values, when none of us were living there anymore, this innocence of the Canadian patriot when we were just as corrupt as any other industrial society."

But Cockburn had an audience in 1972, and it included those who saw the films he worked on. In 1970, he had written the soundtrack to Canadian film director Don Shebib's *Goin' Down the Road*. "Going to the Country," from Cockburn's first album, provided an inspirational starting point for Edmonton filmmaker Tom Radford, who first heard Cockburn perform in Edmonton in 1971. Cockburn provided the sound track for Radford's *Ernest Brown — Pioneer Photographer*, which included the title track from *Sunwheel Dance*. Bruce's music, says

Radford, echoed the rediscovery of the land that many young
Canadians were celebrating.

Cockburn's interest in Christian themes at the time was not
unusual in the world of popular music. Two albums that sold
well that year were *Godspell* and *Jesus Christ Superstar*. But it is
difficult even to begin to compare these high-budget musicals
and their slickly produced albums with Cockburn's understated lyrics and acoustic sound. Neither was Cockburn's social conscience out of the ordinary for 1972. It was the year of
the *Concert for Bangla Desh*, a live album that featured Bob
Dylan, Leon Russell, George Harrison and Ravi Shankar.
Again, however, there were few similarities between the gritty,
outspoken political statements of George Harrison and the
gently ironic aphorisms of Bruce Cockburn. Cockburn's lyrics
were more consciously poetic than those of other popular
musicians writing at the time, born out of solitude and contemplation, not from the psychic din of a large audience's
adulation.

Most young Canadians sympathized with the social ideals
that Cockburn espoused in his writing. Not nearly as many
went out and bought his albums. Kostash has written a book
on the sixties generation, entitled *A Long Way from Home*. In a
conversation with me, she commented on Cockburn's place in
the era of the late sixties and early seventies: "A lot of his
audience admired the man, but his music didn't really do
anything for them, compared to what else was available."
Those who liked acoustic instruments and a folk flavour to
their music were listening to Cat Stevens' *Tea for the Tillerman*
which had been released in 1971. For those who, like Bob
Dylan, had turned from folk to electric rock, there were many
other popular records from which to choose.

The lifestyle that Cockburn advocated was an important
part of his musical style and personality, but many members
of the counterculture were no longer interested in it by 1972.
"There was something about that persona that no longer fit,"
says Kostash of that period. "October 1970 was already two
years back. The program of the counterculture had been
devastated, but Bruce was still playing the part of the wilderness poet." For many, the values of self-reflection, personal
freedom and non-conformity Cockburn was writing about
were laudable enough. Many found his consciously poetic

lyrics refreshing. But it was the "wilderness poet" mask be-hind which he was writing they found cloying. Perhaps as a result, he had only a cult following until 1975 when his audience began to grow.

A Loner's Point of View

Bruce Cockburn was born in Ottawa on May 27, 1945, and grew up in a suburb of Ottawa. His ancestral roots are Scottish. He spent the first year of his life with his mother only, because his father, a doctor, had been in the medical corps sent to Europe after the war. Cockburn says his father "understood very clearly the negative side of human nature. The thing that was missing in that outlook was that people can really shine." Cockburn says he didn't grow up in a religious environment, but that his parents took him to the United Church to please his Presbyterian grandmother. "My parents," he says, "were not particularly politically or religiously involved." Early in life, however, Cockburn sensed "another side of life," a per-ception that has shaded every aspect of his life and career. Commenting on a trip to Nepal on behalf of OXFAM in the spring of 1987, for example, he described the foothills around Mt. Everest as being "crammed with elemental spirits just barely held in check by the efforts of the lamas who live in the monasteries that dot the mountaintop."

As a child, Cockburn coped with his spiritual sensitivity by seeking solitude. It is a pattern he has maintained throughout his life. He has expressed his feelings in this regard most articulately in "Loner" from his album *Inner City Front*: "I'm always living and I always die/ on the event horizon of your eyes/ I'm a loner/ with a loner's point of view." Song-writing for Cockburn is a solitary act, and when he talks about priming the creative process, he refers to a need for "headspace." His bands are made up of what he calls "mercenaries," sidemen who join him for a tour or an album or perhaps both. "When you work with the same people for too long," he explains, "on the one hand it's great because you develop a really fast work-ing language but at the same time you tend to settle in to certain musical habits that need to be shaken up every now and then."

At school, Bruce studied a bit of clarinet and trumpet before getting his own guitar in grade ten at the age of fourteen. He recounts the story of how he found an old guitar in his grand-mother's attic and couldn't put the instrument down. His parents insisted that if he were to play he must take lessons. In addition to taking guitar lessons, he took six grades of Royal Conservatory piano and private lessons in composition. He listened to jazz guitarists Herb Ellis and Gabor Szabo and jazz pianist Oscar Peterson. He learned Les Paul songs and other pop tunes. He copied rock-and-roll licks and solos, imitating Buddy Holly, Richie Valens and Elvis Presley. But towards the end of high school he turned to folk music.

After reading Jack Kerouac's *On the Road* and the work of other Beat writers such as Allen Ginsberg and William Burroughs, he went to Norway and then France, from which he was deported for playing music in the street without a licence. Between 1964 and 1966 he studied theory, composition and arranging at the Berklee School of Music in Boston. In the US, he learned to be grateful he was not an American and to understand the difference between Canadians and Americans. "Protest songs," Cockburn said in an interview with Kostash, "can only be sung within the experience of anger. Because they can feel anger about America, Canadians can sing them without being absurd."

According to Cockburn, John Lennon and Bob Dylan showed that the popular songwriter could be a poet. He says he considers the roles of poet and popular songwriter to be different only in degree: while the concerns of both are identical, the songwriter must, to the extent that he feels possible, tailor his work to popular taste. This is a process that Cockburn has embraced in varying measure during his creative career. "Call It Democracy," for example, is a bitter criticism of the International Monetary Fund and those countries that support it. The song could hardly be less popular in some areas of the United States. "Guerilla Betrayed," when performed in concert in Italy, was quite simply a dangerous act of defiance.

Still, Cockburn's music is for popular consumption. His albums come complete with singles, some more suitable for popular air-play than others, but all aimed at a large audience. The sales speak for themselves: of Cockburn's eighteen albums recorded over a period of more than twenty years, seven have reached "gold" status, having sold over 50,000 copies. Some have sold many more than that. *Dancing in the Dragon's Jaws* has sold over half a million copies. Cockburn's album sales have been boosted by the 1971 CRTC ruling that Canadian music must constitute thirty per cent of AM radio air-play. This was not the only government initiative by which Cockburn was able to advance his career; he was the recipient of a Canada Council grant early in his career.

In a *Globe and Mail* interview, Cockburn once said that he writes to reconcile contemplation with action, just as Christian mystic Thomas Merton did. But he went on to qualify that statement: "I think I have not so much something to say as a way of saying things that works, which means I should say things." For Cockburn, "saying things" means making a political statement or denouncing hypocrisy and hate as it manifests itself in his daily life.

The quintessential comments on Cockburn's music remain those of Katherine Gilday of the *Globe and Mail* in 1978. Gilday's comments summarize the kind of natural imagery Cockburn has used so skilfully and poetically, and she suggests the transcendent purity that is at the heart of Cockburn's poetic vision. In her estimation of Cockburn's music as filled with "stars and streams and blue space," she also names "a yearning for purity and wholeness" as the single unifying emotion in Cockburn's lyrics. The fear and panic that are the flip side of Cockburn's imaginative world must finally give in to the beauty of a universe ruled and inhabited by a benevolent God. It is not surprising that in 1973 Cockburn "broke down and admitted" that he was a Christian. For the same reason, he would later take an active interest in the writings of Charles Williams, a twentieth century English poet, lay theologian and novelist. Williams' literary universe was one in which the forces of order, truth, and beauty always conquered those of chaos, hypocrisy, and evil.

The portraits on the cover of Cockburn's albums are telling: they may be mugshots (*In the Falling Dark* and *Waiting for a Miracle*) or, as with many of the earlier albums, they may show him somewhere in the wilderness. He is always alone. He steps onto the public stage only when he decides he wants to, in contrast with the managed appearances of other popular music performers. Interviews are given sparingly (about one for every ten requests), and are given to promote albums, publicize a chosen humanitarian cause or, very rarely, to gain the minimum amount of publicity needed to keep his career going. The visual aspect of all the albums is thematic. The circle, the globe, the image trying to break out of the medium, and Cockburn's intense gaze, always projected with his face tilted slightly away from the camera's lens. *Big Circumstance* features all of these. The visual impression of all the albums taken together is of a path, a spiritual journey.

Poet of Promise

Self-reflection and contemplation are the mark of a literate man, and Cockburn is literate, in both his art and his interviews. If he is a rocker he is one of the few literate practitioners. His lyrics are written to be heard. They are an expression of thought, emotion and sense, not a denial of these, as other rock lyrics are. As a result, Cockburn as rocker disappoints some listeners. Rock is characterized by an expression of the expansive self, of love as cage or prison or disease, of the attraction and power associated with speed and endless motion. Occasionally, a rocker will dabble in pseudo-religious imagery in an effort to write "subtle" lyrics. But rockers are generally not interested in a view of the universe from anything other than the first person. Cockburn, on the other hand, sings about selflessness, about love as truth, and about unity and wholenesss. His lyrics are pensive, poetic. The idiom of rock works against Cockburn.

If Cockburn's is a literary art, so were much of the rock lyrics of the 1960s: T. Rex was influenced by Blake; the Beatles — Lennon in particular — by the Beats and William Burroughs; Bob Dylan even took his name from a poet. The new wave and punk artists of the early 1980s also acknowledged the influence of poetry on their work. Until the beginning of his foray into rock in 1981, Cockburn rarely mentioned other musicians as influences, only poets and writers. He even resorts occasionally to spoken lyrics ("If a Tree Falls," for example). It's a sign of the failure, at times, of the idiom of popular music to express his ideas.

In Cockburn's poetry, from 1969 to present, we are shown a vision of a universe in which a breach has been torn between man and God; we are also offered the metaphor of human love for divine love. "Are no men/is only Man seeking one love" he writes on his first album. On World of Wonders (1985),

Cockburn presents the haunting portrayal of the poet assuring Providence that "we're doing okay down here tonight." On *Inner City Front* (1981), we are shown the pitiable image of man spinning uncontrolled on the "rim of the galaxy"; we ourselves are the "break in the broken wheel." "The world's in convulsions," he cries on *Sunwheel Dance*. These convulsions are not physical manifestations, however: "the weather is fine/ buicks get bigger and five cents costs a dime."

Cockburn's albums can be considered in groups of three, each group being characterized by a particular aesthetic and personal identity that Cockburn adopted during the recording of those albums. *Sunwheel Dance*, released in 1972, was the last album Cockburn wrote using the persona of the happy hermit. With *Bruce Cockburn* and *High Winds White Sky*, the album forms a trilogy that contains the nascent forms of what would become, on later albums, brilliant and inspired songs. "Going to the Country," for example, the first song on *Bruce Cockburn*, has such forgettable lines as "Look out the window, what do I see?/ cows hangin' out under spreading trees." But the song's first person narrative from a moving vehicle will be brought to life in the frantic chant of "Silver Wheels" on *In the Falling Dark*. "The Bicycle Trip" mentions the "Eternal Dancer," an archetypal figure who will be reborn first in "Lament for the Last Days" and then in "Hoop Dancer," a cut that Cockburn wanted to record for an album with ECM, the prestigious German free jazz label. The project never materialized, but the fact that ECM was interested showed how far Cockburn had progressed in his song-writing abilities since his first album.

"Love Song" on *High Winds White Sky* is another example of an early Cockburn song that held the promise of his future writing. Here, he uses human love as a metaphor for divine love: "In the place my wonder comes from/ There I find you." It is a poetic device that is echoed in the poignant "What About the Bond" on *Humans*, in which the decay of human love is put for the decay of divine love: "What about the mystical unity/ What about the bond/ Sealed in the loving presence of the father."

On *Sunwheel Dance*, Cockburn turned from the descriptive nature poems of his first two albums and instead used his imaginative power to make sense of natural phenomena. In

"Life Will Open," he writes that we are "busy dreaming ourselves and each other into being" and that "we are children of
the river we have named 'existence.'" The lyrics are among the
finest of his nature poems and represent the culmination of
Cockburn's vision of nature as a portrait of the inner state.
"Fall" poignantly recites the beauty of an autumn day and
hints at the rebirth that must follow death. In "Up on the
Hillside," the first of Cockburn's suggestions of apocalypse
appears: "You and I, friend, sit waiting for a sign."

On his next three albums, beginning with *Night Vision*, released in 1973, Cockburn exchanged the face of happy hermit
for that of travelling troubadour. Now the city's buildings and
people, which until *Night Vision* had not appeared in Cockburn's songs, became a source of imagery. "Déjà Vu" is a
triptych of the poet's view of his world ("glass café faces"), his
art ("slow lines on pages"), and his subject ("sun on hair dancing"). The song is remarkable for its poetic unity, a quality that
would find its most eloquent expression in "How I Spent My
Fall Vacation" on *Humans*.

The second of this group of three records, *Salt, Sun and Time*,
includes "All the Diamonds in the World," a devotional piece
that expresses Cockburn's vision of religious ecstasy as experienced through physical sensation. It is a motif that appears
throughout Cockburn's lyrics. In "Man of a Thousand Faces"
(from *Bruce Cockburn*), for example, a man tries to find in
nature answers to his spiritual questions: "surf of golden
sunlight/ breaking over me/ man of a thousand faces." In
"Sahara Gold" (from *Stealing Fire*), the spiritual dimension of
sexual love is suggested: "half moon shining through the
blind/ paints a vision of a different kind/ and your hair
tumbles down like sahara gold." But in "All the Diamonds,"
Cockburn's quiet, lilting voice and acoustic guitar accompaniment achieve a simplicity of expression that haunts even the
most cynical of listeners. Cockburn still includes it as a main-
stay of his live performances.

On *Joy Will Find a Way*, released in 1975, Cockburn
continued to explore the spiritual dimension of human relationships. In "Hand-Dancing," for example, two lovers' play-
fulness is put for the idea of spiritual union: "Song swaying in
the air/ I'm hand-dancing in your hair/ You're hand-dancing
in my soul." In "Starwheel," the slowly changing night sky

suggests that love, which also must change, is the standard against which man's life must be measured: "we're given love and love must be returned/ that's all the bearings that you need to learn." The most poignant expression of Cockburn's vision of spiritual love is found in "A Long-Time Love Song." Here, the poet's powers fail ("words fragment and fall") but are renewed in the hope of resurrection: "You know I long to see that sail leaping in the wind/ And I long to see what lies beyond that brim."

Cockburn sees in nature the images of divine love, as each verse in "A Life Story" illustrates: "Sky-wild/ far cry/ wing-slash-free/ Christ is born for you and me." The comparisons between natural images and religious ideas will be developed to its highest level in *Dancing in the Dragon's Jaws*, an album that contains such evocative image clusters as this one in "No Footprints": "crossed sticks lie on earth/ between crossed sticks — pile of ash/ something rises on the wisp of smoke/ dog's feet move by fast."

The Christian Ecstatic

In the Falling Dark, released in 1976, is the first album that is strongly unified by musical and lyrical motifs and by distinctive instrumentation. With the next two studio-recorded albums, *Further Adventures Of* and *Dancing in the Dragon's Jaws*, *In the Falling Dark* forms yet another trilogy of albums, now characterized by the persona of Cockburn the Christian ecstatic. Midway between the wilderness and the city — he had rented an apartment in Toronto — Cockburn finds a clarity and balance of expression that is not found in his previous albums, with their simple lyrics and collage of musical styles, and that will not be repeated in his later albums, with their sometimes frantic lyrics and Cockburn's strained style of rock.

"Silver Wheels" is a good example of the change of perspective in Cockburn's lyrics since the last album, *Joy Will Find a Way*. The "shimmering spaces" of "A Long-Time Love Song" become the "black earth energy receptor fields" of "Silver Wheels." The "chiming bells and shining curls" of "Lament for the Last Days" are replaced by "muzak sound track to slow collapse." "Gavin's Woodpile" is the least poetically successful of Cockburn's attempts to marry his social conscience with his lyrics. Inspired by a session cutting wood at his father-in-law's country home, Cockburn took the opportunity to reflect on the plight of the inmates at Manitoba's Stoney Mountain Penitentiary, where he had performed with other musicians in 1975.

Further Adventures Of contains the remarkable "Outside a Broken Phone Booth with Money in My Hands" that begins with the startling line that depicts some coins as emblems first of the universe and then of the crucifixion: "I've got planets in my palm — there's a red smear on the sky." As he did on *In the Falling Dark*, Cockburn combines biblical allusion ("Young men see visions and old men dream dreams") and ecstatic experience ("everything is thunder under the celestial waterfall"). The last line summarizes the ideal state for the mystic: "you get close enough to real things — you don't need yourself at all."

In the Falling Dark was the first album released widely in the US. For many Americans, an ashen-faced Cockburn peering from the cover was their first encounter with him. One critic called the lyrics "apocalyptic." "They [Cockburn and Jackson Browne] have chosen to look with death in their eyes over the modern slag heap toward the Millenium," wrote Bart Testa in *Crawdaddy*. On the cover of *In the Falling Dark*, Cockburn certainly has "death in his eyes," but the album's first cut, "Lord of the Starfields," is more apostolic than apocalyptic. Two literary influences can be mentioned in relation to the lyrics of this song. First, a quote by Blaise Cendrars, whose poetry Cockburn had read: "… writing is burning alive, but it is also to be reborn from the ashes." In the song's plaintive refrain, Cockburn echoes Cendrars' view of the role of the poet and names the source of the poet's inspiration: "O love that fires the sun keep me burning." Second, the poetry of Bliss Carman, a Canadian who was writing at the turn of the century, makes for interesting comparisons with Cockburn's lyrics, although Cockburn says his recollection of Carman is confined to high school studies. Here are some lines from Carman's "Lord of My Heart's Elation," written in 1903: "Lord of my heart's elation,/ Spirit of things unseen,/ Be thou my aspiration/ Consuming and serene." Cockburn's depiction of God as an omniscient overlord of the wilderness is similar to Carman's depiction, and places him in the company of those Canadian poets who have sought to define Canada by exploring the psychic effects of wilderness.

Dancing in the Dragon's Jaws, released in 1979, is at once a peak and a point of departure for Cockburn. Every song on the album is an ecstatic testament to his vision of a spiritual life. Nature is a source of imagery on the album, instead of a mystical entity to be praised and idealized, as it was on the first three albums. Rock, sea and sky are the visual cues for Cockburn's thoughts of eternity. Beginning with the next album, *Humans*, he writes of a shattered ideal, of the chaos that is a result of the collision of ecstasy and evil. The albums after *Humans* are characterized by hard-edged social commentary and expressions of anguished love. This change in Cockburn's style would coincide with the abrupt dissolution of his relationship with Kitty, his wife of ten years.

The glimpse of perfect ecstasy, power, freedom and beauty that Cockburn saw in nature and wrote about in his early songs echoes the theme of the writings of Charles Williams, whose work Cockburn read at the time he was writing the songs for *Dancing in the Dragon's Jaws*. In the liner notes of that album, Cockburn mentions his indebtedness to Williams for influencing his lyrics. For a popular musician, Cockburn was citing a very "literary" influence, reflecting Cockburn's sustained interest in the written word as the starting point for his creative projects. Actually, the seeds of the images and symbols found on that album had been planted much earlier. Cockburn had used the image of the Holy Grail which, in Williams' *War in Heaven* represented a passage between this world and the next, in "Lament for the Last Days" (from *Joy Will Find a Way*): "O Satan take thy cup away/ For I'll not drink your wine today./ I'll reach for the chalice of life/ that stands on Jesus' table." As well, the religious ecstasy of Williams' *Shadows of Ecstasy* is hinted at in "Keep It Open" (from *Bruce Cockburn*): "When thoughts rush by/and your signals seem to fly/keep it open."

Musically, the arrangement of the acoustic instruments on *Dancing* provides an integrated sound, utterly suitable to the lyrics. Cockburn had certainly established a distinctive sound by 1979. That sound would change over subsequent albums, but never again would he record a mixed bag such as *Night Vision* or add incongruous material, as he did when he included "Nanzen Ji" on *Further Adventures Of*. "Wondering Where the Lions Are" became a hit in Canada and the US. It was his first song to get top forty air-play. As a result, *Humans* attracted much attention from American critics.

Cockburn and the "Idea of America"

Until 1975, Cockburn refused to tour the US in support of his albums, two of which had been released in the US by Columbia's Epic label. As a result, Epic dropped Cockburn in April 1974 (it began releasing Cockburn's albums again in 1987, beginning with *Waiting for a Miracle*). Then, in 1976, Island Records obtained the True North catalogue, and Cockburn's albums, beginning with *In the Falling Dark*, were again released in the US. Cockburn explained his reasons for avoiding US tours in an interview published in the *Winnipeg Free Press* in 1978: "For a period when I was getting started I went to New York to check things out. I found out that I'd have to lick a lot of boots and hang around in an ugly environment to get anything going and I didn't feel it was worth it."

Cockburn chose to live and work in Canada largely out of a mistrust of the United States. His response to the aggression and competitiveness he saw in the US was to withdraw. Kostash says that "he got a really good scare in Boston. For someone who was trying to set up contemplative space around himself, the United States wasn't going to be the source of his art." Occasionally, such as on *Joy Will Find a Way*, the anti-American sentiment would surface in his lyrics: "Yankee gunboat come this way/ Uncle Sam gonna save the day/ Come tomorrow we're all gonna pay." In an interview with the *Montreal Star*, Cockburn, in referring to American politics, linked the apocalyptic imagery of his lyrics with his fear of the US: "If you give a crook power over you he's gonna do crooked things and you're gonna suffer.... The way I approach the whole thing is that the whole thing could just blow any minute. I don't see any point in running around and screaming at people." In Kostash's article, Cockburn links his fear of the city — articulated so clearly in "Thoughts on a Rainy Afternoon" from his first album and repeated by him continually until 1980 — with his fear of the US: "The more Canadians fill up their space," he said, "the more they will be like Americans. We seem to take it so much for granted. Perhaps because our urban landscapes are not yet deadly, and because they seem accidental to the whole expanse of the land."

Cockburn's manager, Bernie Finkelstein, has expressed frustration that, at Cockburn's insistence, the US tours are not as long as they could be. However, the effect of Cockburn's ambivalence to the "idea of America" has not been confined to the length and nature of his tours. If spiritual freedom is the main subject of Cockburn's writing, the "idea of America" is its opposing force. For Cockburn, the United States represents symbolically those forces that would bind the human spirit. Poetically, the symbol has appeared in other forms in Cockburn's songs (Toronto, the policeman, in his earlier writing), but no force has been as obvious in his writing and personal life as that of US nationalism as it expresses itself in foreign policy. "There are all kinds of things about American society that are inimical to the exercise of spiritual freedom," he says. Although those forces may be found elsewhere in the world, they are nowhere more immediate for Cockburn than in the United States.

The fact that Cockburn is Canadian has been a source of interest for critics, both Canadian and non-Canadian. Other Canadian artists have experienced the same attention to their country of origin. But for Cockburn, his Canadian identity has often been cited as a possible explanation for the mysticism of his lyrics. *Rolling Stone* called him the "Mystic from the North." *Crawdaddy* called him "Canada's Dark Knight" and went so far as to try to illuminate Cockburn's lyrics with the statement that "Canada itself is a nation resting in an unconscious vision." In fact, Canada's collective vision is no more apocalyptic than any other country's. Admittedly, geography and natural setting are prominent in any nation's art, and this accounts for the Canadian artist's portrayal of a looming wilderness and man's struggle to survive in it. And certainly Cockburn's music, especially since 1980, has expressed the anguish of the poet's solitary vision. But this is not unique to Cockburn or to Canadian musicians. Folk-rock musicians to whom Cockburn is compared — Nick Drake, John Martyn — have written with more intensity of the mystical and solitary nature of poetic experience.

What is distinctively Canadian about Cockburn's music is its self-conscious style. Cockburn's lyrics are not a rambling catalogue of images that Bob Dylan might offer; they are not crafted poems in the style of Nick Drake; and they are not the intoxicated chant of John Martyn. They are, rather, a transformation of these, a result of the distance that Cockburn has set up between himself and the forces he sees as being antagonistic to his spiritual freedom. His music, as almost all critics agree, defies categorization. We can trace the stylistic strands of Cockburn's influences, but Cockburn has a remarkable ability to change a style and make it his own. In his lyrics, he absorbs a literary or poetic influence and changes it, whether it is Williams' grail imagery or the controversial views of American theologian Harvey Cox. The self-conscious style — the attempt to withdraw from the vortex of the larger political and cultural forces in which Canada finds itself — is certainly not unique to Cockburn, but Canada has never seen a popular songwriter achieve that distance with such personal and professional success. Cockburn has developed his musical and poetic style with each album and maintained, to the extent he has chosen, a loyal following of listeners.

That critics find it difficult to categorize Cockburn's music helps to explain the fact that they inevitably compare his songs to those of other artists: "I get compared to everyone from John Lennon to John Denver to U2 to Bruce Springsteen (because I happen to share a first name with him). In the pop music media scene, there's a terrible need to categorize everything. Everything has to be sold according to its category and marketed along certain lines." If at any given time he is asked whether he has in mind the personnel for his next album or the plans for a video, he will almost certainly say no, because these are considered only after the songs have been written. This is in marked contrast to the carefully constructed market strategies devised by the producers of popular music's brightest stars. The "direction" for the single, album and video are decided, then the serious writing begins. But for Cockburn the written word is the starting point for, not a byproduct of, his creative work.

In the Spotlight: Cockburn's World View

On a fall night in 1987, I went to hear Bruce Cockburn perform solo in Edmonton. Using only two acoustic guitars, a Chilean instrument called a *charango* on "Santiago Dawn," and a set of wind chimes, he kept a sold-out crowd enraptured for two hours without an intermission. It had been several years since

Cockburn had appeared solo. When he is accompanied by a band, his voice and the artistry of his guitar playing do not shine as they do when he is alone. But what impressed me most that night — I've seen him in concert several times — was his ability to keep an audience with him for the entire performance. The audience senses his personal and artistic integrity — he would never say or sing anything false or affected — and allows him to maintain complete control of the concert. Even when he begins to stray towards preaching, as he did in an introduction to a new song called "Gospel of Bondage," his listeners know that whatever Cockburn says is backed up by the experience of the heart.

Here was Cockburn, his voice and world view fully matured, singing a fifteen-year-old song, "All the Diamonds," and having the audience react, not with nostalgia, but with a sense that the song could still evoke an emotional response. His onstage persona that night was reminiscent of the one he created in the late 1970s. Then, as on this night, he kept the between-song banter to a minimum, strumming his guitar occasionally as if to underline his image as a man in thought. When he was interrupted by an exuberant fan, Cockburn stopped strumming.

"I beg your pardon?"

"The acoustic sound," the fan said, "is great."

The crowd cheered. Cockburn, bashfully: "Well, thank you."

Many of the old songs were reintroduced, including "How I Spent My Fall Vacation," "Lord of the Starfields," and "Tokyo." None were selected from the first few albums and none were from *Inner City Front*. The awkward and shy Cockburn occasionally came through. He walks with his head slightly hanging; his shoulders are hunched. You only notice it when he walks offstage. He encouraged everyone to sing on two songs that defy "singing along": "Nicaragua" and "Dust and Diesel." Still, it is when the spotlight covers him that he becomes truly eloquent. The earnest dialogue and the shyness that characterize his one-on-one encounters disappears.

The "Big Circumstance" he sings about on the album of that name is the calling to write and perform the music. On the back of the *Big Circumstance* cover is what looks like a silhouette of a record and a model of a globe that Cockburn seems to be trying to hide behind, and on the dust jacket, the inevitable result of the "Big Circumstance" is revealed, of course, as Cockburn's loss of privacy. There is a half-tone image of Cockburn in the disguise he uses when walking around Toronto, the baseball cap and the down-turned eyes. Cockburn is a perfectionist who has chosen a lifestyle that guarantees a generous amount of chaos. He is a craftsman in an art form peopled with hacks. He is a sensitive soul who has chosen to live in a world of competition and cruelty.

Cockburn has written songs in many genres, including blues, reggae and folk ballads. His writing over the last few years has been marked by driving rock rhythms and sometimes frantic lyrics. A short-list of Cockburn's best, however, would include songs that feature his own musical style: "All the Diamonds in the World," "Lord of the Starfields," "No Footprints," "How I Spent My Fall Vacation," and "Waiting for a Miracle." All are visions of paradise, expressed through the use of a unified set of images, some from nature, some from the city, set to music characterized by solid form, by Cockburn's unquestioned virtuosity as a guitarist, and — always — by the spare, impassioned voice, sweet in its untiring proclamation of faith and all that is beautiful.

Bruce Cockburn — The Best

Song: "All the Diamonds"

Album: *Dancing in the Dragon's Jaws*

Article for further reading: Myrna Kostash, "The Pure, Uncluttered Spaces of Bruce Cockburn," *Saturday Night*, June 1972, pp. 21-24

Discography

Bruce Cockburn (1969)
High Winds White Sky (1971)
Sunwheel Dance (1972)
Night Vision (1973)
Salt, Sun and Time (1974)
Joy Will Find a Way (1975)
In the Falling Dark (1976)
Circles in the Stream [live] (1977)
Further Adventures Of (1978)
Dancing in the Dragon's Jaws (1979)
Humans (1980)
Inner City Front (1981)
Mummy Dust [compilation] (1981)
The Trouble with Normal (1983)
Stealing Fire (1984)
World of Wonders (1985)
Waiting for a Miracle [compilation] (1987)
Big Circumstance (1988)

6·The Importance of Being Murray

Do you dream of being somebody
So the world will love you
— "Do You Dream of Being Somebody"

Backstage at the Edmonton Folk Festival, that haven of peace and all things folkful, a man of rank within the Festival's organization decided it would be a neat idea to throw a piece of meat at the man who had penned the words and music to "The Farmer's Song." The projectile was, as I recall, a slice of roast beef. Murray McLauchlan, perhaps himself having tossed a cold-cut or two in his life, seemed neither offended nor shaken by the incident. With tongue in cheek, he up-braided the man and then continued his conversation with me. *I* was offended and shaken. Surely, I thought, the act of writing a ballad of the stature of "Whispering Rain" would entitle a songwriter to some measure of respect. Apparently not.

McLauchlan has spent twenty years or so following a cycle of repeatedly departing from, and returning to, the sources of his musical and lyrical ideas: the abrasion of the inner-city street, the milltown and its grey skies and, as a psychic an-tidote to these, the northern wilderness. In the engagement with these sources McLauchlan has occasionally discovered creative energy, even inspiration. Occasionally, he has allowed the star-making machinery to stifle his creative energy, but he has always had the ability to find a path back to the sources of his art. Such artistic determination confirms his stature as a popular musician of distinction. The results of these points of engagement — represented most clearly on the albums *Song*

from the Street, Boulevard, Timberline and *Swinging on a Star* —
reveal McLauchlan at his best. In his recordings and performances, McLauchlan strives to create a mood, an effect, for his
audiences, and this is in keeping with the traditional role of
the folk singer-songwriter.

Murray Edward McLauchlan was born in Paisley, Scotland,
on June 30, 1948. If you should meet him on the street, you will
assume I don't have my facts straight — because a man who
looks thirty cannot be over forty. And cowboy boots and the
hint of a drawl are not native to Scotland. Yet who in the world
of Canadian popular music is what he seems? Certainly not
Murray McLauchlan. He has been called the quintessential
Canadian folksinger. He writes about Canadian heroes, legend
and myth. He has also been — in the words he has used in
referring to his reclusive colleague, Stompin' Tom Connors —
"vilified and laughed at."

When McLauchlan was five, his family moved from Scotland to Canada. At seventeen, he began playing at coffee-
houses in Toronto's Yorkville area. While attending Toronto's
Central Tech as an art student, he decided to become a musician. After a foray into the New York scene, McLauchlan came
home and began recording for True North, owned by Bernie
Finkelstein. This arrangement lasted until 1987, when he
signed with Century City Artists.

McLauchlan has earned several Junos; he has written music
for television and film, most notably the television special
"Floating Over Canada" and the feature film *Alligator Shoes*.
He has also starred in two acclaimed CBC radio series: *Timberline*, an aural exploration of Canada's north, and *Swinging on
a Star*, a showcase for singer-songwriters. In addition, he has
contributed to charitable projects by writing the theme song
for the International Year of Disabled Persons (1981), serving
as Christmas Seals Chairman of the Canadian Lung Association (1984) and helping with the recording of "Tears Are Not
Enough," for Northern Lights for African Relief Aid (1985).

The Limits of Success

Two writers who have provided lucid and insightful examinations of McLauchlan's work are Bart Testa (now with the
Department of Cinema Studies at Innis College in Toronto)
and Myrna Kostash (an Edmonton writer). Testa wrote a piece

reviewing Gordon Lightfoot's *Gord's Gold*, McLauchlan's *Only the Silence Remains*, and Bruce Cockburn's *Joy Will Find a Way* for a funky, albeit hard-to-find, magazine called *Crawdaddy* (June 1976). Kostash wrote a comprehensive profile of McLauchlan for *Saturday Night* in 1977 after riding McLauchlan's tour bus for a few days. Each article came to very different conclusions about McLauchlan's stature as an artist. This is because Testa was observing McLauchlan in close contact with one of his all-important artistic sources — in this case, the life of the working man — while Kostash, writing a bit later, was finding out what happens when McLauchlan finds himself estranged from these sources.

In his article, Testa attempted to place his subjects in a kind of "history of popular lyric ideas." Thus, if Lightfoot was the maker of myths and Cockburn the herald of the apocalypse, McLauchlan was the poetic Everyman. He was an observer of all that is wrong with Canadian society. Coming from a working-class family (his father, he told *Rolling Stone* in 1978, was an iron turner for most of his life), he could not forget the fine edge of social injustice the blue collar worker must negotiate to maintain his or her dignity. McLauchlan's poetic observations, according to Testa, were characterized by a "humane and pained" panic, the kind of terror that comes of seeing the world for the first time as it really is. But out of this terror he was not able to fashion an organic and creative response. Instead, Testa wrote, "Murray McLauchlan has stayed at the center of his realism, his regionalist observation and his political-moral posture." Even so, this was no small feat, Testa pointed out, considering the output of many popular musicians at the time; this was the year, after all, of Captain and Tenille. McLauchlan's music was raw and imposing, even attractive; his audience was growing.

Kostash, on the other hand, saw McLauchlan as a personification of the dilemma that becomes apparent in any thorough social analysis: he was no more an exploiter of the capitalist system than he was a victim of it. Followed around the continent by an entourage that included a manager and any number of marketing and press hangers-on, McLauchlan kicked back in the only way he knew how. He repeatedly changed his persona, his poetic mask, so that his pursuers never found out who he really was. After a personal encounter between writer and singer, Kostash was able to brush some of these masks aside: "The confusion of motifs I had been bewildered by in his environment — star, businessman, macho punk, populist poet, broken-hearted clown, balladeer of doomsday — clears up when I see him as a man whose real life goes on, surely and self-consciously, behind the phantasmic screens of publicity that are, after all, only useful."

The perspectives of Testa and Kostash — of McLauchlan as realist poet on the one hand and as tired rocker on the other — are separated only by a year or so. Testa predicted the North American market push that would follow the release of McLauchlan's live album *Only the Silence Remains*. Kostash observed firsthand the western Canadian leg of that push. The differences between the two portraits can be traced to McLauchlan's attempt to increase his artistic scope from that of folk singer-songwriter to that of international pop superstar, an effort that met with only partial success. McLauchlan's artistic and commercial success in song-writing has consistently been proportional to the intensity of his contact with what for him are elemental experiences: working, loving, travelling.

The narrow range of McLauchlan's emotional themes is not in itself a limitation. A singer-songwriter's lyrical powers are based on the skill of observing or imagining an emotional state and transcribing it with clarity and poignancy in the shorthand of the popular song. By "popular song," I include all the styles in which McLauchlan has dabbled: folk, rock, rhythm and blues and country. McLauchlan understands the main limitation of his medium: three or four minutes is normally the maximum time allowed for a song. Real time is used to measure these creations, rather than the number of verses or words, because radio play is the key to financial success in pop music. And this is the limitation that drives all of the conventions of popular music: the rigid form (instrumental introduction, three or more verses with refrain), the ensemble (almost invariably a solo voice with two or three back-up singers) and, most important, a memorable phrase, word or idea. McLauchlan has often been able to fashion strong musical structures, given the limitations of the popular song.

Furthermore, his musical ability is unquestioned. He plays piano and guitar with equal sensitivity and skill. These instruments figure prominently in most of the arrangements. For a good piano performance, listen to "Immigrant" on *Hard Rock Town;* for guitar, "How Many Times Can a Fridge Break Down" on *Storm Warning.* And his harmonica playing — he plays the harmonica better than anyone working in mainstream popular music — is heard on most songs, a kind of symbol of the singer-songwriter's solitary pursuit. Still, one critic has called McLauchlan's musical style "dog-headed." Technically, it is accomplished by the use of a limited number of chords, generally the three "I, IV, V" chords common to rock and country music; occasionally, he uses minor and secondary chords. The general pattern of his progressions is characterized by a great deal of repetition, even by popular standards. The accompaniment is almost invariably played on an acoustic instrument or two: piano and guitar and perhaps a slide guitar or harmonica. There are exceptions: *Boulevard* and *Hard Rock Town* have an uncharacteristically high proportion of electric guitar, and *Storm Warning* and *Windows* feature a disco sound. But in general, McLauchlan has repeatedly returned to the simple, direct style of writing and arranging that has characterized his most successful songs.

For some songs, however, McLauchlan's instrumental abilities are not enough to sustain the lyrics. For example, while "Horses on the Highway," from *Timberline,* contains a very poetic motive — this century's transfer of brute power from animal to machine and the mythical echo of the sound of hoofbeats to be heard in the roar of semi-trailer trucks — the title phrase is simply repeated too often. McLauchlan often doesn't develop the main idea of a song to the point that the song becomes viable. "Best Foot Forward," "Jealousy" and "Try Walkin' Away" suffer from the same flaw.

His most musically and lyrically successful *recent* songs are based on the same aesthetic as that of his earliest songs: the use of a simple vocal and acoustic instrumental structure within which the most important element, the lyrics, is framed. The best of his lyrics, as I have mentioned, deal with a few important themes. The criterion for high quality is the success of the music in somehow illuminating, dramatizing or foiling the emotional content of the words. The thing to listen for in McLauchlan's songs is the effect. This intention to create an overall experience for the audience is confirmed in

McLauchlan's tendency to name his compositions simply "songs": "Child's Song," "The Farmer's Song," "Old Man's Song," "Train Song."

Defined in this way, "Child's Song," from his first album, remains a complete success, even after repeated listenings. The musical accompaniment consists of nothing but the gentle changes of an acoustic guitar. The chords include major seventh intervals, which in the musical language of folk often suggest poignancy and a sense of loss. A meditation on a child's passage to independence, the song touches on family, home and memories. The singer regrets the moments of anger in his past, but is resigned to the passing of all things: "We all just got too old to say we're wrong." As a poem, the thoughts expressed would come across as syrupy, overly sentimental; as part of this song, they constitute an important element of the means by which the effect on the listener is created. A song like this either "touches" you or it doesn't; most listeners are touched.

"Whispering Rain" is another song in which McLauchlan finds his powers as a singer-songwriter. The chord progression is unsophisticated and the accompaniment simple. McLauchlan's voice is uncharacteristically hushed. The refrain suggests the same sense of lost love that works so well on "Child's Song": "Whispering rain, careless emotion/ Rising and falling waves on the ocean/ Carry you home 'til nothing remains/ But the sound of the whispering rain." In short, there's nothing remarkable about either the music or the lyrics. But taken together they accomplish McLauchlan's emotional intent. In particular, the restatement at the end of the song of the piano's imitation of rain — that curious, tentative triplet riff first heard at the very beginning — is among McLauchlan's most tender effects.

Between 1971 and 1974 (from his first album until the release of *Sweeping the Spotlight Away*), McLauchlan was able to create a body of songs that explores the loves and losses of middle-class North America. His narrative stance is that of the observer and commentator. It is, in short, the accepted stance of the folk singer-songwriter. Accordingly, these four albums are characterized by a folk style; the lyrics are refined and economical, as they must be in the folk idiom. The prototypical song for this stage of McLauchlan's career is "Down by the

Henry Moore," the first cut on *Sweeping the Spotlight Away*. The memorable lines from the refrain, with their reference to flight and ecstasy and McLauchlan's growing fame (as the writer of "The Farmer's Song"), encapsulate McLauchlan's concerns as a folksinger: "Don't you want to keep on moving/ Don't you want to get undone/ Don't you want to change from losing/ Don't you want to have some fun."

The Glory Years

Many folksingers were trying to get a foothold in North America in the early 1970s. McLauchlan stayed in Canada and persevered. He can only have benefited from the Canadian content regulation for radio air-play which took effect in January 1971. The regulation called for thirty per cent Canadian content between the hours of six a.m. and midnight. Ritchie Yorke notes in his book on the Canadian rock music industry that a recording with Canadian content was defined as any composition that fulfilled one of the following: the instrumentation or lyrics performed principally by a Canadian; the music composed by a Canadian; the lyrics written by a Canadian; or, in the case of live performances, recorded wholly in Canada. Since 1971 was the year McLauchlan recorded *Song from the Street* (his first album), "Honky Red," which appeared on it, undoubtedly received more air-play than it would have, had the regulation not been in place. "The Farmer's Song," which appeared on *Murray McLauchlan* and which was released the following year, enjoyed the same benefit. Ironically, some internationally successful Canadian musicians — such as Gordon Lightfoot and David Clayton Thomas — have said that such requirements harm, not help, Canadian musicians. They argue that when a foreign (including American) radio program manager or record executive looks at sales figures or air-play statistics on a given Canadian musician, he or she discounts the figures as a matter of course, since it can be assumed that at least part of the musician's success can be attributed to the content regulation. As a result, the manager may choose to give the musician's work less attention than it deserves. In the case of McLauchlan, however, since his success abroad has been limited, content regulations have been of benefit to him.

The early 1970s were the glory years for McLauchlan. The songs he wrote in this period, such as "Down by the Henry Moore" and "The Farmer's Song," remain his calling cards. In fact, McLauchlan was still singing "The Farmer's Song," which remains his best known song, when he appeared on *Sesame Street* in 1989. (He joins the ranks of other popular Canadian performers such as Buffy Sainte-Marie and Andrea Martin, who have also appeared on the show.) But a folksinger generally attracts only small audiences. Because folk songs only occasionally "cross over" into the pop or country charts, their potential for air-play is limited. With the release of *Boulevard* in 1976, McLauchlan attempted to gain wider appeal. It seemed quite possible: in the US that year, Linda Ronstadt, with her slick blend of country and pop, released the very successful *Hasten Down the Wind*. McLauchlan's music took on the sound and trappings of rock, while maintaining certain folk and country concerns: acoustic instruments remained at the centre of the arrangements, and the lyrics continued to deal with folk issues, although they were now oriented to the mill-town, rather than to the inner city.

McLauchlan was following a trend that was evident in Canadian society generally. It seemed that year that those without a voice might just kick out the jams. It was the year of Justice Thomas Berger's Mackenzie Valley Pipeline Inquiry, which was to change the way politicians — and Canadians generally — thought about the north and its people. There was a mood in the country that minorities, even powerless ones, were on the ascendancy. McLauchlan's developing theme of celebrating the working class seemed right for the time. By 1978, when he spoke to *Rolling Stone* magazine, McLauchlan was still talking about the political *rightness* of his music, even though he was about to abandon its artistic usefulness soon enough: "If there are to be any fundamental changes in the way business or government treats people on this continent, that realization is going to come from the working class."

The Silver Tractors, with whom McLauchlan recorded and performed at the time, made the transition to a rock sound artistically possible. A group of experienced side-men, the Tractors gave musical marrow to McLauchlan's compositions. On *Boulevard*, for example, the Tractors made their influence felt by providing a strong musical framework for McLauchlan's songs. Ben Mink's violin and Gene Martynec's electric guitar, for example, give a sense of drama to "Getting Harder to Get Along"; the drumming by Jorn Anderson throughout "La Guerre C'est Fini Pour Moi" musically evokes the military atmosphere suggested by the lyrics.

The Tractors perceived the essence of McLauchlan's talent: the courage to expose the raw nerve of emotion. For such an exposition, they sensed the need to keep the musical framework uncontrived and potent. To do this, the band slowed down McLauchlan's tempo a bit, giving the songs a sense of powerful repose, something that seems to be missing when session musicians have been brought in for some of McLauchlan's other albums. There is also a sense of assurance and steadiness on *Boulevard*. Most importantly, the band helped McLauchlan establish and follow a particular musical direction; they developed a channel for his creative energy, which would later dissipate without the Tractors.

Boulevard includes one of McLauchlan's best songs: the title cut, an ode to the working class called "On the Boulevard." The song's success is based on the deft expression of a simple but poignant scene, that of weary workers on a Friday night reborn to the life of the street. Another song on the album, "As Lonely as You," may be considered a study for the beautiful "Whispering Rain" (which would be recorded three years later), with which it shares a similar rhythm, introduction and emotional atmosphere.

Hard Rock Town was released in 1977, after McLauchlan's tour of Japan with Bruce Cockburn. One of the songs is a lesson in contrasts of the way two songwriters respond to the same experience. Cockburn's "Nanzen Ji," from his album *Further Adventures* (1978), is a set of three haiku-like verses set to music. The mood is serene, the lyrics spare and sweet. This was Cockburn's reflection on Japan. McLauchlan's "Sweet Song of Asia," on the other hand, speaks of human bodies and filth: "Drinking up hard liquor/ While the TV pattern hums." Of course, Cockburn would release quite a different song in 1980, the popular "Tokyo," a song about the other side of Japanese society. But the comparison remains useful. For Cockburn, the appeal of Japan lay in the contemplative distance he observed in some aspects of Japanese society; for McLauchlan, it was in the heat and energy of the city, in the passions of the working man. When McLauchlan returned to Canada, he found that the experience had changed him, as he told *Canadian Composer* magazine: "Everyone [in Canada] looked so big and stupid and gangly and awkward, and everyone was so *rude*. It took quite a while for me to realize that I was all those things too."

Hard Rock Town also features the especially beautiful "Immigrant." Ben Mink's violin parts are masterfully arranged and performed. It is a very short song (three minutes), but it accomplishes that all-important *effect* that McLauchlan has kept at the centre of his artistic intentions.

But in spite of the band's accomplishments with McLauchlan, it was sent home in the middle of a concert tour in 1976. The reason: McLauchlan's transition to rock was not attracting a large enough audience. *Hard Rock Town*, released in 1977, is the last album to feature the Silver Tractors.

Leaving aside a compilation and live albums, his next two albums, *Whispering Rain* (1979) and *Into a Mystery* (1980), feature a grooving McLauchlan. The highlights are "Whispering Rain" and "Nassau Town" on the earlier album and "A Thousand Miles Behind" on the later one. Both albums were uneven in their artistic success, but they continued McLauchlan's attempt to find a place on the rock map.

Into a Mystery features background vocals by Carole Pope (of Rough Trade fame), a label-mate of McLauchlan's. Having Pope singing on such cuts as "Try Walkin' Away" gives the songs a ribald effect they would not have had otherwise. This is a result, not only of Pope's distinctive voice and her vocal habits, but also of the association the listener makes with Pope's own repertoire, which included "High School Confidential" — a song about male adolescent sexual anxiety, written in the first person. Sung by a woman, "High School Confidential" took on an ironic tone and became a parody of all similar rock treatments of the subject.

Pope's appearance on the album raises the question of the artistic development and control that can be discerned in McLauchlan's output. The musical arrangements on any of McLauchlan's albums are usually indistinct from one another and, for that matter, from the arrangements to be found on any number of albums by other singers. Piano, guitar, harmonica and slide guitar are the most common instruments used. In a typical song, there is an instrumental eight-bar introduction. There are three or four verses, each of which has a chorus. The chorus almost invariably includes a phrase or line that is repeated within it several times. Examples of this kind of phrase include "thousand miles away," "trying to stop the sun from going down," "highways in the sky," "swinging on a star." An instrumental passage might provide a break between the third and fourth verses. At the end, the instruments play some kind of reprise of the introduction.

The repetition that is characteristic of McLauchlan's songs is common in folk, pop or rock songs. What is unusual is the fact that over a period of almost twenty years of composing, performing and recording, nothing suggests that McLauchlan's lyrical or musical skills have *changed*. They haven't withered or died; on the other hand, they haven't flowered. Occasionally, on one of the albums something or someone will be introduced to provide some kind of break from what has gone before. On *Boulevard* and *Hard Rock Town* it is the sound of the Silver Tractors; on *Into a Mystery* it is the voice of Carole Pope. What is missing from McLauchlan's work is a genuine progression of ideas and artistic gestures. Such development is not necessarily the sign of a great singer-songwriter, but it often accompanies the efforts of the best. It provides for an artist a path from which reference points may be taken for the purpose of planning future efforts. Without it, an artist can make big mistakes, as McLauchlan's next couple of albums demonstrate.

Losing (and Finding) the Path Home

On *Storm Warning*, released in 1981, and *Windows*, released the following year, McLauchlan lost his way. The albums illustrate the hazard of lacking a sense of musical direction, something the Silver Tractors had been able to provide for McLauchlan through the recording of *Boulevard* and *Hard Rock Town*. Both *Storm Warning* and *Windows* include a large portion of disco offerings, complete with pretentious arrangements and McLauchlan's nervous voice. The lyrics are overcharged and sometimes silly. In particular, "Jealousy" (from *Windows*) features a disco introduction, followed by the silliest lines McLauchlan has ever sung through clenched teeth: "Doctor, doctor, won't you help me please/ Got this feeling I don't need/ Jealousy/ Hey hey hey." Perhaps part of *Storm Warning*'s failure can be attributed to its producer, Bob Ezrin (who had worked with Pink Floyd previously). Presumably he had been hired to add some marketing whiz to McLauchlan's material. But it is clear that McLauchlan had strayed from what, for him, are authentic themes and had taken up, instead, prefabricated pop themes. The only note to add about *Windows* is that it includes what is almost certainly one of popular music's most asinine songs, a composition entitled "Animals."

After the *Storm Warning/Windows* diversion, McLauchlan returned to the musical style that had worked best for his voice and for his lyrical sensibilities — a blend of country, folk, rock and rhythm and blues. On the satisfying *Timberline* (1983), the theme is one of McLauchlan's favourites, that of the northern wilderness. McLauchlan's harmonica, which he plays with passion on all his albums except *Storm Warning* and *Windows*, returns as a confirmation that McLauchlan has left behind the tracings of those albums. After playing a riveting harmonica solo in "Storybook Love," McLauchlan sings lines of startling passion: "We've fought to a standstill/ We grind ourselves dry/ I just can't stop loving you/ I can't even try." On this album, produced in conjunction with the CBC radio series of the same name, McLauchlan found his way again. Canada's north gave McLauchlan the artistic touchstone needed to create something meaningful after the poor showing of his previous two albums. Perhaps he was following the lead of his hero and fellow bush pilot, Max Ward, who, when in need of mental and spiritual recharging, has often retreated from the metropolis to a remote northern cabin, where he can see and feel the essence of what was once the main adventure of his life: open spaces, the danger of a harsh climate, and time for contemplation. McLauchlan's own avocation as a pilot has led him to explore — both geographically and musically — the heroes of Canada's aviation history. His album *Heroes*, for example, is a collection of songs dedicated to various heroes of McLauchlan's, two of them pilots.

McLauchlan says he sees his radio series *Timberline* and the television special "Floating Over Canada" as somehow making a contribution to Canadians' awareness of their heroic history. What appeals to him about heroic figures is their "taste for adventure," as he explained when I asked him about Max Ward,

Grant McConachie and Wop May, three of Canada's legendary bush pilots: "They did adventurous and heroic things like bringing serum into a community in the middle of an epidemic. Those were the romantic days of derring-do and expert flying." "Out Past the Timberline" sets the mood for all the songs on this album: mystery, isolation, the exigencies of tide and trapline: "Canada is somewhere out there/ Out past the timberline."

After the release of *Timberline*, McLauchlan turned to celebrating the lives of Canadians who were able to transcend the alternating monotony and fear of their lives. The songs of *Heroes* (1984) are a result of McLauchlan's effort to write about other ways of seeing things, but always from a remote perspective. In spite of McLauchlan's vicarious position as observer, the songs are relentlessly direct in capturing an emotion.

Midnight Break (1985) represented the end of McLauchlan's collaboration with Bernie Finkelstein, the owner of True North Records. The songs seem like one last attempt to crack that North American rock market. While the title of "Suppertime in the Milltown" might suggest that McLauchlan was going to return to an examination of the theme of working class pain, the song features McLauchlan — in Billy Idol voice — singing about, yes, escaping from the nine to five. Only "I'm Best at Loving You" gives a hint of the mood of McLauchlan's next album, which would be released three years later.

The Human Cycle of Funk and Grief

Swinging on a Star is a collection of songs in which McLauchlan's voice is steady and warm; there is no attempt to rock or groove. As a result, the album is one of McLauchlan's most successful. The sound is easy country and western, tinged with that pop edge (or lack of edge) that has marked McLauchlan's best songs. The instrumentation and arrangements suit McLauchlan's songs well, with the harmonica riffs that have become a hallmark of his recordings and performances. One quirky aspect of almost every cut on the album is the mismatch between the introduction and the rest of the song. There is a curious irrelevance to each of the intros that can rankle. The title cut has that spiritual twist that marked McLauchlan's earliest work: "I pray with this melody where you wish to be is close to where you are." It is a remarkable song, given what McLauchlan has written before. The song speaks of the small comforts and moments of peace that can illuminate a lifetime, of those glimpses of light that give poignancy and perhaps meaning to the human cycle of funk and grief. "Swinging on a Star," along with the others on this album, represents a moment of peace in a collection of songs, written over two decades, that at times suggested an emotional landscape of fear.

My impression of dualities was confirmed when I met McLauchlan. His eyes, a remarkable translucent blue, convey the restlessness of his personality. His demeanour is intense. When I talked to him, he wanted to begin his answers to my questions by clipping off the ends of my words. It is hard to avoid the sense that he has suffered in some way that he has been unable to resolve even through his music. After decrying the "anti-art" forces at work in the music industry, he said, finally, "I hate the music business."

But if he is candid in his interviews, he also relishes the twists of phrase that make for good copy. As a popular musician, he has many opportunities to indulge himself. Consider the description of working class Canada he gave to writer Stephen Holden: "Sudbury's typical of a lot of Canadian towns. You have a big mill or a big mine in the middle of the town that's destroyed any other means of making a livelihood. You have a captive labor force living in a place that's essentially run on corporate money. Any time somebody makes a noise about anything, they lay off 3,000 employees. Then nobody makes a noise anymore." Exaggeration? Perhaps. Still, you have to admire McLauchlan's punchy style and his courage for using his position as a musician to express his views on social issues. Let's not quibble with numbers. Directness is a virtue in popular music.

And McLauchlan's songs are nothing if not direct. Since they are not set in the strait-jacket of the traditional folk idiom, the way chosen by such musicians as the late Stan Rogers, there is always the possibility of surprise — the quirky reference or metaphor. McLauchlan's songs do not have the psychic reverberations of a Siberry song or the dramatic flair of a lang song. Rather, they have the structure of the storyteller's art. And each story is told from the perspective of the solitary singer-songwriter.

Perhaps the best clue to McLauchlan's ideas of how his music accomplishes what it does is to be found in a couple of lines taken from "Nassau Town," a cut on *Whispering Rain*. First, "Life is a strange kind of song," he writes. It is a summary of the folk notion that a good song somehow not only communicates an idea and expresses an emotion but also, by its very form, reflects the human cycle of life and death. Second, the song makes reference to the folksinger's truism that writing and performing constitute in themselves a form of self-discovery: "I take my guitar and try to make sense from all of the things going down." For McLauchlan, art and life have borrowed from one another. When this exchange has worked as it should, the result has been artistic and commercial success. His release in December 1989 of the single and video "Let the Good Guys Win," featuring McLauchlan and fellow Canadian singers Tom Cochran and Paul Hyde, shows that McLauchlan's creative efforts can still yield artistic success. Perhaps he will continue to dabble in media other than recorded music: he had a small part as a singer named Wild Jim Coady on an episode of *Street Legal* in the 1988-89 CBC television season.

What Murray McLauchlan has done, then, is to remain, after two decades, as he began: a folksinger. He is the only Canadian folksinger among his contemporaries who still regularly performs at Canadian folk festivals. Certainly his credentials as a folk performer are impeccable. He made his first important appearance at the Mariposa Folk Festival in 1966; by 1973 he was performing at the Philadelphia Folk Festival along with Sonny Terry and Brownie McGhee, and Jim Croce. He has been shrewd enough to realize that his forays into disco, or other musical areas for which he has only half a heart, have served only to discount his musical strengths. What keeps McLauchlan's audiences coming back is not his musical originality or poetic sensibility, but his guileless effort to capture in a song the edge of his emotions. Usually that emotion is anger, but occasionally it is something else. Nancy Erlich, writing in *Billboard*, put it this way: "McLauchlan's ability to crystallize the pain in a painful situation is nearly frightening."

In 1966, *Variety* said Murray McLauchlan had potential. Ten years later a feature article in *Saturday Night* talked about the "hype of his current reputation as a Canadian superstar on the verge of international (read American) success." And ten years after that, the *Globe and Mail* said simply that McLauchlan's was "quality music, casually offered." McLauchlan's career represents the cycle of regeneration characteristic of both art and nature. It is a process that he himself has touched on in the lyrics of *Day to Day Dust*. The best of McLauchlan's songs are sketches, executed with economy and intensity. None of them are completed portraits, with the layers of poetic resonance and meaning that accompany fully fleshed lyrical treatments. As a result, the number of themes to be explored is limited. McLauchlan has chosen them carefully: lost or dishonoured love, the ecstasy of flight or escape, and the worker's angst. That's the list. To have maintained a career of more than two decades on such slender sources is remarkable in itself. To have written some very moving and evocative songs along the way is cause for celebration.

Murray McLauchlan — The Best

Song: "Whispering Rain"

Album: *Boulevard*

Article for further reading: Bart Testa, "Royal Canadians," *Crawdaddy*, June 1976, pp. 69-71

Discography

Song from the Street (1971)
Murray McLauchlan (1972)
Day to Day Dust (1973)
Sweeping the Spotlight Away (1974)
Only the Silence Remains [live] (1975)
Boulevard (1976)
Hard Rock Town (1977)
Greatest Hits [compilation] (1978)
Whispering Rain (1979)
Into a Mystery (1980)
Storm Warning (1981)
Windows (1982)
Timberline (1983)
Heroes (1984)
Midnight Break (1985)
Swinging on a Star (1988)

7·Very Siberry

something about this old earth
and the way it looks from up above
*   — "Something About Trains"*

Maybe it was because the day, Holy Saturday, was a venerable one — but the Jane Siberry concert I attended in 1988 was an epiphany for me. I was moved by Siberry's use of dramatic gesture, the understated visual cues she used to frame her performance. The props that night were simple — for one song Siberry stood on a chair — but they gave a sense of occasion, of dramatic intent, to her performance. Since the demise of Motown, choreography has generally fallen out of favour with rock audiences, but throughout songs such as "Ingrid and the Footman," Siberry and her backup singers gestured and swayed to the rhythm of their music with a grace that I had never before associated with rock. The music was good, too, although I couldn't make out most of the lyrics. I was hearing almost all of the songs — taken from her most recent album at the time, *The Walking* — for the first time.

Here was a songwriter who had succeeded where many had failed, in the attempt to fuse the ethos and energy of rock with the diversity and reflection of high art. Jane Siberry has made a valiant attempt to foil the commercial "fact" of her chosen art form by taking a vigorously individualistic approach to writing music and lyrics; like Bruce Cockburn and Leonard Cohen, she has adopted the creative role of the poet.

It is no small achievement to cast off the trappings of a male-dominated art form: at the concert I attended there were none of the shenanigans to exploit the phallic suggestiveness of the microphone stand, for example (the singers wore head-set microphones), and no false emotions or contortions. My impression was that this was *rock by a woman*, complete with mock clothesline hanging above the stage, an image taken from lines in "Lena Is a White Table": "there's a house (white)/ a back porch (grey)/ just a table there/ (don't forget the laundry line)." The clothesline visually underlined the theme of the tour, which was "Flap and Fly," taken from a reference in "The White Tent the Raft."

Admittedly, there were some disagreeable moments that evening. The concert had begun late. Band member Ken Myhr, who plays guitar with avant-garde jazz groups in Toronto and also plays classical guitar with a chamber music ensemble, came out and provided distraction for the audience, playing psychedelic "epic" things on his guitar and then announcing an intermission. At the end of the concert, Siberry seemed impatient with the enthusiastic response of the audience, refusing to play more than one encore. Still, I always tell people who haven't heard Siberry to go and see her live before deciding whether they want to listen to her recordings. Siberry acknowledges that her concerts have a dimension that cannot by conveyed on the albums: "One thing that makes people understand the songs better is seeing where there's irony, or where there isn't, just through the way I move or express things, with a different edge in my voice. I think that's easier for people to pick up live than on record."

The Composed Life

Jane Siberry was born Oct. 12, 1955, in Toronto. She started writing at seventeen, for an English project in school — a significant recollection for her, given her interest since then in lyrics as poetry. For several years, she sang in a trio called Java Jive in Guelph, a group that included John Switzer, who would become Siberry's bassist and co-producer, and with whom she would have a romance for several years. Siberry and Switzer are largely self-taught, musically. Siberry's skills on guitar are not remarkable; her voice is thin but adaptable to the fluid structures of her songs. But the other band members defy the stereotype of the rocker who begins his career by simply buying an instrument and starting to play. Guitarist Ken Myhr and keyboard player Anne Bourne studied music at York University; drummer Al Cross at McGill University.

Perhaps because of the difficulty people have in defining what genre Siberry "fits" into, she has played often at folk festivals, such as the ones held in Winnipeg and Edmonton, even though her songs, other than those on her first album, are inspired no more by folk than they are by rock. It's no use trying to classify her: she has created her own style. Her music represents an approach to music that treats a song as simply one aspect of artistic expression. Siberry incorporates *other* aspects — drama and dance — into her live performances.

A clue to the essence of Siberry's music is a statement by Switzer that her songs begin, not with a musical riff or part, but with an idea. For example, the literary inspiration for "Seven Steps to the Wall" was Arthur Koestler's *Darkness at Noon*, which is about a man in solitary confinement who is facing execution. Sometimes, however, the impetus for a song is visual, as Siberry told *Canadian Composer*: "I'm using the medium of music and lyrics but a more direct way to do it would be to paint or take a photograph or do a movie." "The Valley," for example, from *Bound by the Beauty*, was inspired by the twenty-third Psalm, which Siberry says she had often read to her grandmother; the song is also a reflection on where she lives, the view from which she says reminds her of a corridor, a valley. Switzer explains, in a column he wrote for *Canadian Musician* magazine, that when it comes time to tour and the band must work with limited instrumental resources, they begin with the same idea that inspired the recorded version of a song: "Originally we began with the essence of the story and we told it using everything available to us. Now, live on stage, we have different things available."

If Siberry's primary strengths are a poetic sensibility and a concern with the ambiguities of language, she has tried to acquire whatever musical skills needed to accomplish her artistic purposes. She has dabbled in piano, French horn and guitar. At Guelph University, she enrolled in the music faculty but soon abandoned formal studies. Still, even well into her career she was occasionally taking voice lessons. Even though she is not a "musician's musician," her gifts as a composer are obvious. She is able to conceptualize a particular sound she wants and to gather whatever resources she needs to create that sound. In an interview with *Canadian Composer* magazine, Siberry confirmed her desire to use singers — in addition to words, instruments, gestures — as paint strokes from a palette: "For me sidemen are vehicles to get what I want…. If someone asks me to do vocal work, I want to know what the song means and the feeling they're trying to get, and be their tool." In the same article, she said, "No one really can get what you want as well as you can yourself."

Even on her tours, she is able to gather around her musicians who can help her accomplish what she wants. For the "Flap and Fly" tour Rebecca Jenkins, for example, provided the dramatic flair needed for some of Siberry's songs. (Jenkins would garner critical acclaim in her own right in her starring role in the 1989 Canadian feature film *Bye Bye Blues*.) Similarly, Myhr and Bourne provide the connection with the twentieth century "serious" musical tradition. Many of music's greatest innovators have had the quality of creative leadership without the benefit of outstanding musical skills or training: Miles Davis, John Lennon, Duke Ellington. By intuition, such composers know what they need to learn (the picture of Siberry struggling alone with a book about synthesizers comes to mind), and they are not particularly concerned with their musical forebears or with contemporary influences. They are more or less single-minded in the pursuit of their own ideas.

Siberry's music is not musically complex, but for popular music it is remarkably fresh and full of character. "I Muse Aloud" from *The Speckless Sky* has a 5/4 time signature, which is extremely unusual for a popular song. The easiest way to try to follow the pulse of the song is to think of groups of two two-beat measures, with the second measure of each pair extended by one beat: 1-2, 1-2-3; 1-2, 1-2-3; and so on. Many of her other songs include an occasional change of time signature within a song. She has said that she uses alternating time signatures and fluid tempos because that is the way people talk: "If you heard someone talk who writes really consistently formalized pop songs, I'm sure you'd find that their speech patterns would speed up and slow down; it's very rhythmic and harmonious to their minds. And if they were really writing music in accordance with themselves, they'd probably do that too."

In composing, Siberry says she sometimes uses "free recording," the musical equivalent of "free writing." The revision and refinement processes come later, often with the involvement of her band. Siberry is able to conceptualize a song and record it using a four-track tape recorder and drum machine. Siberry's recordings evoke an all-important mood, the creation of which she has repeatedly named as her prime artistic intention, as she did when she discussed her video "The Bird in the Gravel" in a 1988 *Billboard* article: "People seem to be unnecessarily confused by the song.... They think it's more complicated than it is. It's really not a story so much, but more about a feeling and ambience — a moment." I suppose if Siberry were a jazz composer or a writer of "serious" music, she would be called an impressionist. She continually evokes, conjures, suggests. Her own comments on her lyrics confirm what audiences feel when they hear her, as she told *Melody Maker*: "There seems to me a logic to defining something by the things around it, by leaving an absence there in the middle of the picture. It seems to me that's how you can best convey how people are in a state of poignancy." Siberry says that disorientation — the feeling you get when you're lost in an unfamiliar city — can be a creative force: "I like the sense of being lost," she told *Melody Maker*. "I'm always trying to throw myself into things where I don't have any orientation." Examining "The Lobby," Steve Sutherland of *Melody Maker* came to conclude why so many Siberry songs are about the breaking up of a relationship: "It's the only time people are truly *alive*, thrown into uncertainty, robbed of routine, adrenalized, deprived of another in whom to reflect and rationalise any reactions." For her part, Siberry says feeling lost while composing can actually contribute to the mood of a song: "It's a creative position to be in when all your reference points are removed. I like that. You have to scramble. You have to be like a warrior. It's a poignant state."

Preserving an Artistic Voice

It is not every rocker who would talk about "poignant states." Many are too busy competing for a share of the market to spend time reflecting on the state of their souls. On the various television shows featuring music videos, the hits jostle for the position of "number one." On CBC television's weekly *Good Rockin' Tonight*, for example, there is a countdown of the top twenty hits on every show. For those "in the business," including the performers, agents and promoters, *Billboard* provides an accounting of the recent major performances in the US, stating the artist(s), venue, date, gross income and ticket prices. Siberry seems alienated by the competitive nature of the popular music industry: "It saddens me to see [competitiveness in popular music], because it doesn't really have anything to do with where the best kind of music comes from, which is from a connection between you and yourself." She attributes part of her ambivalence in this regard to the power of commercial radio to influence so many people at a time: "Commercial music is a very small part of a huge stream of creative energy. It makes me feel sad that for some people, commercial radio is their only idea of what's artistic. It's such an unhealthy medium, because the tendency is to make things similar, not make things unique."

Siberry is adamant about not writing exclusively for the commercial pop market, about preserving her artistic voice. In an interview with *Saturday Review*, she said that, with reference to the hit "One More Colour," she told her record company "not to expect another one." The danger for her is that she will fail to keep the pop audience that allows her to continue to record and perform. Neither *The Walking* nor *Bound by the Beauty* included more than one or two songs in the style of "One More Colour," the single that helped boost *The Speckless Sky* to Canadian gold-record status. "Ingrid and the Footman" was designated the single for *The Walking*; for *Bound by the Beauty*, it was the title cut. If she continues to sit on the edge of popular music she will have to continue to include songs that maintain pop accessibility, songs like "Red High Heels." Even though the structure of "Red High Heels" is more complex and experimental than that of most other pop songs, the refrain is easy to remember and pleasant. (Still, who would have thought the quirky "Mimi on the Beach," Siberry's 1984 hit from the album *No Borders Here*, would have had the extensive air-play it did?)

Siberry's first album, a self-titled 1981 release not generally available anymore, is characterized by a folk sound, complete with acoustic accompaniment and vocal backgrounds. While the album is difficult to find and has only a tenuous stylistic relationship to the rest of Siberry's albums, it is a delightful collection of songs. The mood of most of the songs is that of serenity and joy. But it is the lyrics that arrest. They confirm that from the beginning, Siberry's ability to fashion a unique creative voice has its roots in the poetic. "The Sky Is So Blue," for example, is a whimsical song about escaping from the city on a sunny day. It has the kind of off-beat imagery that Siberry would later develop into poetry: "My heart it is so big/ I can't get through the door." The first cut, "Marco Polo," *sounds* like a characterless ballad, until you begin to listen to the words, which express the ambivalent emotions of a woman who is waiting for the famous explorer to come courting."Writers Are a Funny Breed," the most artistically ambitious song on the album, evokes the misty conjurings of the late English folksinger Nick Drake and illustrates Siberry's intention to heighten the effect of the solitary, reflective, nature of her art, an aesthetic that holds true regardless of the number of people on stage with her or performing with her on a recording. A close look at the lyrics yields surprisingly subtle effects. The song begins with an introspective section in which the singer observes the silence of "here": "The room around this room hangs on a golden chain." Then, the background vocalists join the singer to chant, "Frozen in time since you went away." The vocalists are a kind of intrusion in what has been a monologue accompanied by a single acoustic guitar. But it is only a musical convention, a technique by which musical and poetic "space" may be opened up a bit. As listeners, we have already suspended belief in listening to the musical expression of an idea: it is only a small step from that point to one in which other people are actually participating in vocalizing the singer's emotion. It is done all the time.

What happens next is hardly conventional. After the singer sings, "Walking through your rooms, I touch your things," the background vocalists intone, "Walking through his rooms, you touch his things." This is not what background vocalists would sing if this were the plain ballad the music might suggest. Background vocalists usually repeat what the singer has sung, or perhaps vary it so that their narrative stance becomes ours, as in "Walking through his rooms, she touches his things." By singing the words they do, the vocalists *become Siberry's voice.* They "close up" the space that had been opened previously and deflect our attention back to Siberry's words. They become her words, actually her voices, for later, when Siberry sings, "That is why I had to come today," the vocalists sing, "That is why we had to come today." All of which is accomplished by a simple poetic trick. It's the kind of conscious use of poetry that was a sign of what Siberry's most successful later songs could accomplish.

On the album, the sound of Siberry's voice is not as intense as it would become on the later albums. There is a big stylistic leap between this album and the next. The first album has no experimental pieces; it sounds like a quirky folk album. The extensive use of synthesizer — typical on a low-budget recording production — is done tastefully. What is clear from the beginning of Siberry's work is that incisive lyrical impulse — the lyrics on *Jane Siberry* are all vivid, fresh, engaging. Although the musical aspect of her craft would simply take longer to develop than the poetic, each song on this album creates a distinct mood. The album features interesting arrangements and singable melodies; the mix is sophisticated but not pretentious for the obviously limited budget. In short, there's no artistic reason why *Jane Siberry*, unlike Siberry's other releases, should be generally unavailable in commercial outlets. It is distributed through Just in Time, a Montreal jazz label, and is available through Siberry's correspondence address, which appears on her albums.

A Poetry Reading Writ Large

The step forward on Siberry's next album, *No Borders Here*, was to be found in its level of musical sophistication. This album has a *beat*. Siberry's music since *No Borders Here* has been characterized by the strong drumming and quickly shifting tempos and rhythms that were first heard on this album. "I Muse Aloud," for example, begins with an instrumental introduction that has much more energy than anything on the first album. It is the song mentioned earlier, with the 5/4 time signature. Similarly, "Dancing Class" features a polyrhythmic section and aggressive electric guitar; its extended form was a departure for Siberry. Although the first album featured some very short spoken passages, "Extra Executives" features Siberry's spoken voice on the entire penultimate verse. Every song on the album is characterized by the potent, driving rhythms and sharply delineated sections that have now become typical of Siberry's music.

"Symmetry," from *No Borders Here*, is the song that caused critics to compare Siberry to American avant-garde singer Laurie Anderson. Comparisons to Anderson have been frequent and heavy for Siberry, to her dismay. But some of the comparisons are apt. John Rockwell's description of Laurie Anderson applies perfectly to Siberry: "The effect [of Anderson's performances] is like a highly attentuated art-rock concert, a stylized lecture or perhaps a poetry reading writ very large indeed, with every aspect of the poetic concept amplified and counterpointed by aural and visual imagery. The subject is herself on one level, but more generally, in the tradition of all autobiographical artists, her observations on whatever it is that is the subject of a given piece." Like some of the cuts on *No Borders Here* — and especially "Symmetry" — Anderson's songs are often characterized by the *Sprechstimme* form of vocal delivery, in which words are delivered in a style straddling song and speech. Anderson, an accomplished violinist and therefore familiar with the conventions of high art music, would have been influenced by the twentieth century German composer Arnold Schoenberg, whose *Pierrot lunaire* featured *Sprechstimme* throughout. The vocal delivery is not the only aspect of "Symmetry" that brings Anderson to mind: the lyrics are arty, associative, "difficult"; they continue Siberry's concern with the poetic.

Siberry's process of raising the level of musical sophistication and, at the same time, making the songs swing, continues on *The Speckless Sky*. "Mimi on the Beach," with its simple accompaniment, became a hit and established Siberry as an accomplished popular composer. But in Siberry's succession of albums, the second half of *The Speckless Sky* is the point at which the listener really gets bogged down in a lot of poetry without the benefit of tune. In particular, "Vladimir — Vladimir" illustrates the problem inherent in the dichotomous path Siberry is trying to follow. Such a song, which aspires to the avant-garde, doesn't belong on an album of popular music. And Siberry's albums, regardless of their vitality and character, *are* popular albums. By including a song like "Vladimir — Vladimir," Siberry disaffirms the album's popular identity. She also underestimates the sophistication of the audience, because she seems to assume that the audience needs to have a broad selection of material on one album. This may allow the musicians to do what they like to do, but it doesn't take into consideration the way people listen to popular music. "Taxi Ride," on the other hand, is a return to the gentle evocation of mood that characterizes Siberry's first album: "Love is a strange thing/ It depends what one gives/ And sometimes to give means/ Give someone away/ Oh, you're sleeping."

"Map of the World (Part II)" is a continuation of "Map of the World (Part I)" on *No Borders Here*. The series skips *The Walking* and continues on *Bound by the Beauty* (titled as "Are We Dancing Now [Map III]"). The significance of this development of the theme of a map is that Siberry's songs, taken together, affirm art as the only human expression that, because of its potential for political and religious neutrality, holds some hope for society. As she told *Canadian Composer*: "I've always resented any kind of arbitrary boundary. And that comes from language. I mean, the borders to countries were articulated by men, and they're not natural boundaries between people. And so I don't think that way, and think of myself not as a Canadian but just as a type of being, and think of other people that way." She agrees with the notion that music is a kind of neutral political ground: "Music is a universal language. It erases differences. Music from the heart is on an inarticulate level. That is, to me, the most moving and attractive thing about music. Often I write about that part of people that works with an inarticulate language. *The Walking* was especially about that, about the language in between, everything in between. It's just as defined a place, but it's more difficult to define." As a result of her views in this regard, Siberry says that taking up political or social causes through the composition and performance of protest songs "makes her nervous." She says she still feels free to speak out on issues, but not through music.

Paying the Price for Critical Acclaim

The Speckless Sky, with its hit "Mimi on the Beach," was the first Siberry album to attain gold status in Canada. After the album's release, the British critics, normally tough nuts to crack, expressed instant affection for Siberry. Kris Kirk of *Melody Maker* wrote, " 'One More Colour,' with its soaring choral passages and its seamless harmonies, was so spiritually uplifting I swear I levitated for a minute." Back on earth, the video for "One More Colour," co-starring a cow, received a great deal of television air-play. That cow was not the first one to appear in Siberry's work. On *Jane Siberry*, "The Mystery at Ogwen's Farm" is apparently about a missing cow named Bessie; "The Strange Well" also has a reference to cows.

The next album, *The Walking*, did not produce a hit, even though the album is considered an artistic success. "The Bird in the Gravel," for example, is an "art song" of stunning effect. Its intricate structure is masterfully conceived, incorporating gesture, sound, and colour. Like Mitchell's "Dancin' Clown," the song is a dramatic sketch. It features eight characters: the master, servant, maid, pantry, Francesco the truck driver, the bird, boy coming home from lesson, and another boy. Each character has a musical identity appropriate to his or her "personality." The servant, for example, who is practising his technique in serving tea ("place the tea just so"), sings alternating intervals of fourths and sixths in a rhythm that suggests an automaton. The maid sings a dreamy incantation: "something's going to change/ i know i know i know...."

All the human aspirations portrayed in the song — the master's lordship, the studied motions of the servant and even the anticipation of the maid — are shown in the light of the glories of a fall day (albeit a fall without the colours of fall) and its symbol, the bird in the gravel. The *moment* that all the monologues move towards is that of the bird's warbling. The song's structure can be imagined as being made up of several layers. Or, it can be considered in terms of the cinematic idiom, with the field of view progressively narrowing from that of the master's musings on his station in life to that of the "bird in the gravel's" song. At the end of the song, the view has widened again to that of the servant rehearsing his technique for his master and to that of the maid in a state of poignant expectation. Musically, it ends with a variation of the instrumental accompaniment of the "Pantry" section, this time, however, in the style of a church organ, recalling the maid's reference to trees crossing in the breeze and "healing bells."

The drama of "The Bird in the Gravel" results as much from the musical tension created by the song's polyphonic effects as from the juxtapositions of the dialogues. When the maid begins singing, for example, the musical effect is as strong as the dramatic effect. While there is no linear narrative (no "story"), each character is delineated in striking detail and nuance. A song that aspires to the artistic level that "The Bird in the Gravel" does is difficult to absorb fully without the aid of a lyric sheet or, for that matter, in one listening. Fortunately, *The Walking* includes a lyric sheet that indicates the juxtaposition of dialogue by placing the characters' lines side by side when they are sung together. For that matter, it is important that the lyrics to the songs on any Siberry album — like those on a Mitchell, Cockburn or Cohen album — really need to be included in a lyric sheet.

"The Bird in the Gravel" must be seen in performance for full effect; like many of Siberry's songs, it is cinematic in its quick cuts and in its visual evocation of a landscape. Interestingly, when *Melody Maker* asked about her musical influences, Siberry responded that she was influenced by, among other people, the Soviet filmmaker Andrei Tarkovsky. She now lives with underground filmmaker Peter Mettler, with whom she is working on an extended video based on the song "Vladimir — Vladimir." (Mettler took the cover photos for *The Walking* and *Bound by the Beauty*.) Siberry has produced her own black-and-white video based on "The Bird in the Gravel," which was sold in videocassette form at concerts.

With *The Walking*, Siberry signed with Warner Brothers for distribution of her albums all over the world except in Canada. (Windham Hill, a "new age" label, had distributed *No Borders Here* in the US.) Since the 1970s, the distribution arms of large American record companies have gradually replaced the independent Canadian distribution companies. The result has been a steady increase in their sales: Paul Audley cites that between 1970 and 1981, the ten largest companies increased their share of total best-selling albums by volume from 79.5 per cent to 99.1 per cent. While many albums are produced by Canadian independent labels — companies such as Duke Street for Siberry and True North for Bruce Cockburn — the distribution is almost invariably carried out by an American-controlled company. Cockburn's distribution in Canada has always been through CBS (an American distributor), but Siberry's is through Duke Street, a refreshing arrangement and one that bodes well for the survival of Canadian distributors.

With all of the success she has enjoyed (a gold record, critical raves), Siberry still has to work hard to keep her career going. In 1988, she told *Canadian Musician* that she was still in debt, in spite of her strong album sales: "I haven't made any money yet from sales, none at all, here or in the US, anywhere." As in book publishing, income for the "creator" in the recording industry is based solely on royalties. Also, regardless of the size of an advance a recording artist receives (the more successful the artist, the larger the advance), the royalties from sales of the album must recoup the cost of production before the artist begins to make money. If the advance is not actually earned by sales, the size of the advance may be smaller for the next album; alternately, the record company might simply tear up the contract to avoid further losses.

Thus, if royalties are ten per cent, *The Walking*, which cost about $100,000 to record (apart from the cost of actually reproducing the discs, CDs and cassettes, which is normally borne by the label), would have to sell almost 85,000 copies (assuming a retail price of twelve dollars) before Siberry would begin to make money. Siberry charges a co-producer's fee, but in the case of *The Walking*, she waived the second half. Then again, recording and production costs vary widely. Murray McLauchlan's *Storm Warning* (1981) was estimated to have cost $120,000; on the other hand, Bruce Cockburn's *Dancing in the Dragon's Jaws* (1979), which went platinum in Canada and which sold very well internationally, cost only $26,000 to record and produce. What all of this means is that there is a financial and personal price to pay for choosing not to write to formula. So far, Siberry has been willing to pay that price.

The Singer as Poet

After the release of *The Walking*, *Melody Maker* published several gushing Siberry articles and reviews. (One of them used the word *genius* every 100 words.) As might be expected, *Melody Maker's* writers were most interested in Siberry's poetic gifts. The best of these articles was based on an interview with Siberry conducted by Jonh Wilde. In it, Wilde mentions the red leaf that Siberry writes about in "The White Tent the Raft": "I tell Jane Siberry that it sounds like everything depends on that happening." Then he makes a connection with William Carlos Williams' famous poem "The Red Wheelbarrow," which can be quoted conveniently since it is so short: "so much depends/ upon/ a red wheel/ barrow/ glazed with rain/ water/ beside

the white/ chickens." It happened that Siberry had been thinking about the poem recently and endorsed its appropriateness
for a discussion of her songs.

Three points of comparison can be made between Siberry
and Williams. First, like Williams, Siberry concerns herself
with an attempt to "reawaken" language. In this sense, her
lyrics are "anti-poetic": in spite of their sheer quantity, the
words are continually retreating from their object, allowing —
actually inviting — the listener to become involved in making
emotional connections. Perhaps this is why Siberry's recorded
voice sometimes sounds as if she is thinking about something
else. The space opened up by this distance can be occupied by
the listener. She describes the process this way:

> People reach out to music so much because they need to
> keep that unique, fantastically curious, and completely con-
> tent part of them alive. People use music as a vehicle or drug
> to get them there. Maybe you could say music is a way of
> waking up that part of people. Most of the time people are
> trained to be the same and flat and deadened, not to be
> themselves. Everyone is a truly eccentric person. But you're
> trained not to be. People crave to be made to feel special, so
> they go to music that makes them feel that way.

Also in common with Williams, Siberry has chosen the
spoken, idiomatic language of popular intercourse as her medium. She observes the mundane events of a human life —
walking, listening, seeing, touching — and uses them as the
subjects of her poetry. In this regard, she has repeatedly stated
that although she is wary of becoming a worker in popular
music's hit factory, neither she does not want to address an
élite audience, and this accounts for her choice of subjects: "I'm
attracted to using everyday things, to keeping things
grounded, like red wagons or shoes or furniture." She calls
herself an "everyman's poet."

Finally — and this is the most compelling of the three points
— Siberry has adopted Williams' aesthetic posture that each
earthly being, object, sensation, and moment is, to use a word
she might not use herself, holy. What I mean is that in her
lyrics, she abandons the subject-object mode of apprehension
in favour of allowing the poetic subject to exist apart from
human experience. Williams, quoted in the *Norton Anthology
of Modern Poetry*, put it this way: "The particular thing offers

a finality that sends us spinning through space...." and "To refine, to clarify, to intensify that eternal moment in which we alone live there is but a single force — the imagination." As poetic observer, Siberry, too, is at once present and absent, first person and third.

Listening to *Bound by the Beauty*, which was recorded shortly after the *Melody Maker* interview, I can't let go of "The Red Wheelbarrow" as an informing power for every song on the album. "The Life Is the Red Wagon" illustrates the most direct connections to Williams' poem. A child's toy as a metaphor for a life shared between lovers reminds one of the red wheelbarrow. The last words of the song call the wagon "simple and strong" — it is the kind of conscious and overt naming of the metaphor that has become Siberry's trademark. The title cut also speaks of the essence — and finality — of "earthness" for human experience. Granite and flowers evoke the grave, but the song suggests the transcendence of death, with the singer coming to life half a millennium from now. "Something About Trains," "Everything Reminds Me of My Dog," and "Are We Dancing Now?" illuminate single moments by finding their connection to some other part of the universal web.

Trains, Hockey and the Human Voice

Bound by the Beauty is less experimental than Siberry's previous releases. The title cut has been released as a single and produced as a video. Siberry says "The Life Is the Red Wagon" will also be made into a video. All the songs have an easily discernible form and, except for "Are We Dancing Now? (Map III)," there is little of the kind of epic instrumentalizing that appears on *The Walking* or *The Speckless Sky*. However, it is still clear that Siberry is determined not to write specifically for commercial radio: none of the songs sounds like top forty material.

By its themes, the album shows that Siberry is finding a place as a distinctly Canadian singer-songwriter. "Above the Treeline" deals with the mystery of the north, a much-used Canadian theme. There is a song devoted to the subject of a kid's game of hockey, similar in mood to that of Joni Mitchell's "River": when Siberry sings the first line of both the opening and closing stanza, the sense of peace recalls Mitchell's song. The album reveals another close link to the tradition of the

Canadian singer-songwriter, since Siberry shows she cannot avoid the influence of country music: "Something About Trains" features an ambling tempo and the familiar country emphasis on the second and fourth beats. Lines like the following, taken from the chorus, could be from a song by Murray McLauchlan or perhaps Neil Young: "But everytime I hear that whistle blowing/ I find myself a-shivering in my soul."

If Siberry has established her own artistic space in popular music, she has also been influenced by her colleagues. Like Siberry herself, I do not find comparisons with other musicians helpful. Occasionally, however, they provide a source of interest. Don Shewey of *Rolling Stone* referred to Siberry's rhythms as "Eastern-ethnic," noting that in this she reflects the influence of Bruce Cockburn. "Half Angel Half Eagle," from *Bound by the Beauty*, really sounds as if it was influenced by the "urban angst" songs of Bruce Cockburn. The lyrics are disjointed and resilient, and the music drives to a rhythmic climax. The voices in unison — half shouting, half singing — also evoke Cockburn's 1980 hit "Tokyo." The link with Cockburn is also a result of the two musicians' common interest in the written word as the creative kernel for a popular song. For her part, Siberry has named her musical mentors (as a composer) as Randy Newman, Tom Waits and Elvis Costello. She also says that Neil Young symbolizes what she is seeking artistically: "People who inspire me give me the courage to listen to myself more, because I sense that they're doing that. Neil Young is someone who inspires me. He's a rebel in the truest sense." As a student of the human voice, Siberry finds Young's voice a source of inspiration: "There's one line at the end of a Neil Young song that I used to listen to over and over again. It moved me so much. Just the funny way his voice fades away."

When I talked to Jane Siberry, she was at one end of a phone line somewhere in Busy City, and I was at the other end, sitting in a little room in a sprawling building at the southern edge of the northern Alberta bush. We had talked about Neil Young, about her parents, about Toronto. I was struck, as other interviewers are, by the timbre of her voice. *Melody Maker* described it as being characterized by an "awkwardly hesitant, forever faltering dysphonia." Whatever it is, it makes a conversation with her seem so *tentative*.

She spoke warmly about her family as an important source of strength: "Part of the courage I have to listen to myself and not be swayed by how the outside world defines me comes from the security of knowing that I have the respect and love of two people, no matter what I do. That's a very subtle thing, but hugely significant for anybody."

When our time was about to run out, Siberry, instead of answering one of my questions, shifted my attention to the conversation itself.

"Marco, your voice sounds very tired," she said.

It was true that I was suffering fatigue at that moment. I was still recovering from a hectic trip to Montreal the week before, and the interview with Siberry had started late, making me feel a bit anxious. But I have listened to a tape of our conversation several times and cannot detect how she sensed my personal state at that moment. I replied that I had been busy lately.

She persisted: "You can't sing and not tune into the human voice. It tells you a lot about people."

It was a perceptive touch to our exchange, very fleeting, very human. Just like that moment of musical drama I experienced one spring night at a Jane Siberry concert — there was a resonance I find hard to forget. Very Siberry.

Jane Siberry — The Best

Song: "The Bird in the Gravel"

Album: *Bound by the Beauty*

Article for further reading: John Wilde, "Flowing Muses," *Melody Maker* 64 (Aug. 6, 1988): 8-9

Discography

Jane Siberry (1981)
No Borders Here (1984)
The Speckless Sky (1985)
The Walking (1988)
Bound by the Beauty (1989)

8·Portrait of the Artist as a Young Cowpunk: k.d. lang

I'm not asking for the world
I just wanna be an ordinary girl

— *"It's Me"*

One summer night in 1982, I was sitting at one of the tables in a community hall of a small town that hugs Alberta's Highway 12 just west of Consort, the village of 650 people in which k.d. lang was born and where she grew up. The occasion was a wedding dance. There were too many people in the hall for such a hot night and, as the hours passed, the blue haze of cigarette smoke thickened. The band was a local country and western combo, playing country standards and occasionally covering a slightly aging pop hit. It wasn't k.d. lang singing, but the influences on lang and on this band were the same, as I found out when I first heard lang five years later.

Well into the evening's festivities, I noticed a couple, probably in their early twenties, entering the hall. They didn't greet the bride and groom. It was a cash bar; no one seemed to mind. Then, the band began to play a polka. Of course, because it was a country and western band, the polka was not authentically eastern European in style: there was no accordion, mandolin or violin. Furthermore, the beat was bolstered by a full drum kit, which wouldn't have been found in a traditional polka arrangement. This was polka *à la prairie*. At this point it became clear exactly why the crashing couple were here — they were here to dance. They began wheeling around the circumference of the dance area at what would have been a dangerous speed if they weren't good dancers. But these two were good. The woman was pressing herself tightly to her partner, whose cowboy boots would occasionally kick up and back in the style that only the best polka-dancers can accomplish. They were a whirling flutter of dress hem and denim, he with his head snapping around to negotiate their way around and around the hall. It was a vision of energy and colour that impressed upon me a rhythmic potency that is not often associated with country and western music.

If k.d. lang's performances have also been marked by the energy and colour of a prairie polka, it was her physical appearance that first caught the imagination of her audiences. The jewel-studded, lensless horn-rimmed glasses which lang wore until 1986 were distinctive, as was her short hair, which she has now begun to wear a little longer. When she toured North America in 1989, she wore a sequined short jacket and tuxedo pants on stage. For a country musician, her appearance is revolutionary, and that's appropriate, because lang has turned the image of the female cowboy singer upside-down.

A Question of Identity

Lang's appeal to popular audiences is a result, not of her ability to "cross over" musically to the pop idiom — Kenny Rogers can do that — but, as she puts it, her success in making light of country music. Her glasses, cowboy boots and dresses are parodic. She gently, but affectionately, pokes fun at country music's most cherished conventions, including stage appearance. This is the way a British writer described an outfit lang wore in a concert warming up for Lyle Lovett, as published in a review in *Melody Maker*: "The article in question was a sky blue cowgirl dress with fluffy white clouds and a big yellow sun, and a little picket fence with some cows chewing their cud round the shoulders, and green fringey bits hanging down. It was, er, quite an eyeful."

While lang's rise as a musician has been meteoric, she hasn't always found it easy to convey her personal and musical identity. For example, in 1989, when she appeared for a second time on *Late Night with David Letterman* (her first career-boosting appearance had been in 1986), she mentioned the Slavic influence in the country music tradition she had grown up with in central Alberta. Some of the audience tittered — *Slavic* influence? If you haven't been to a dance in rural Alberta, the notion of combining Slavic and country elements might seem far-fetched.

In fact, the mixture creates a potent synergy. This is because polka is a close cousin of swing. Both dance steps are based on placing stress on the second and fourth counts of a four-beat (4/4) measure. (A typical rock rhythm, on the other hand, emphasizes the first, third and fourth counts.) A country and western tune with a quick tempo will often also place stress on the second and fourth counts. When the polka influence is added to such a tune, the pace is imbued with new energy, since a straight polka will often end in a tempo much quicker than the one in which it began. As a result, dancing to such music can be a very energetic activity. The *difference* between the polka and swing styles is that swing employs a great deal of syncopation (the avoidance of the beat in the melody), while polka does not.

Part of lang's difficulty in expressing her artistic identity is related to the fact that she's very young. She was born in 1962, and there is a certain gap between the generation that lang represents and that of others she works with, and even that of some of her audience. As a result, people sometimes don't "get" her humour or fully appreciate the subtleties of her musical persona. When she was recording *Shadowland,* for example, she played "Pine and Stew" — a tune that Peter Gzowski called the "quintessential Canadian country tune" — for Owen Bradley, the album's producer. Bradley, who is several decades older than lang, called the song a "novelty," apparently unable to appreciate the co-existence of satire and homage in lang's music.

It is the kind of humour that lang expressed most publicly when she accepted the Juno award for the most promising female singer in November 1985. She bounced onto the stage wearing a wedding dress and then proceeded to make promises (as in a wedding ceremony): she would promise to deserve the award, to work hard, and to "always sing for the right reasons." Most people in the audience didn't understand the barbed gratitude, including one of lang's fans, Peter Gzowski, who, according to lang, said he only finally understood her three days after the ceremony. Lang's humour is the humour of a generation raised on recordings, infatuated with television, and a little less than reverent. It's the humour of *SCTV* and *Ghostbusters*. But to those who don't get it, it can seem silly or even offensive. Lang doesn't mind: "You've got to make the effort, right?" she told *Canadian Composer* magazine in 1985.

It is also the humour of the performance artist, and this raises the most significant of the public facts of lang's life: before deciding to pursue music as a full-time vocation, lang spent time creating and performing as a performance artist. This activity was undoubtedly influenced by her attendance at art school before taking up music, in the tradition of Joni Mitchell and Murray McLauchlan.

What is performance art? Consider Laurie Anderson, perhaps the most successful of contemporary performance artists. Her music, which consists largely of spoken lyrics — some altered electronically — are punctuated, foiled and juxtaposed with instrumental accompaniment. Her work has been called solo opera. The comparisons with lang are tempting. Both use humour (lang is careful to call her humour "Canadian") and visual gags (the horn rims, the wedding dress, the sawed-off cowboy boots). One of the tantalizing aspects of performance art is that it has often been performed in art galleries. Perhaps this is because a performance artist requires a venue where the expectations of a "musical" audience do not hamper the free expression of a hybrid art. One of lang's "happenings" as a performance artist was a song about Barney Clark, a retired sixty-one-year-old dentist from Des Moines, Washington, who was the recipient of the Jarvik-7 artificial heart in 1982. Clark died in 1983, 112 days after the transplant. Lang's tribute was a seven-hour re-enactment of Clark's surgery.

The best token of lang's career as a performance artist appears as the last cut on *A Truly Western Experience*, a song called "Hooked on Junk." Recorded at a plodding pace, the song features lang's voice — now thin and tired — and a single acoustic guitar. The words recount the destitution of an addict. But if Jane Siberry's songs are reflexive, continually turning on themselves, lang's songs emote, extending their possibilities outwards. "Junk," the most stark example of this quality, places the singer in a particular setting, allowing the audience to consider the relationship of artist to environment. It is extroverted music. As *Variety* has put it, lang has "one foot in the avant-garde and one foot in the past." Lang herself has commented on this aspect of her music. In an interview with *Canadian Living* in 1989 , she said, "My music is considered alternative. I bet if I looked the part [of a mainstream singer], it wouldn't be. But I'm doing my music the way I want to. I'm not saying I wouldn't like a hit, but it would have to be on my terms."

The *performance* is thus the most important aspect of lang's art. In her live performances, she is energetic, dramatic and intense. For lang, the overall artistic effect — the costumes, dancing, and vocal pyrotechnics — are more integral to the performance of her music than they might be for a trained, more "musicianly" musician. In fact, anything lang does, on stage or off, is part of the "package": appearing in the stunning "wedding dress" at the Junos; naming her band, the Reclines, after the late Patsy Cline; carefully adopting, then abandoning, the horn-rimmed glasses.

Lang makes it clear that although she was surrounded by country music as a child (as anyone growing up in small-town Canada is), she *chose* it as a career pursuit. "I value what I learned (from performance art)," she told Perry Stern of *Canadian Musician*, "but it was so limitless that there were no boundaries to work within and try to change. That's why I chose country music. It has such a structure that I find the potential to challenge it really exciting." In another interview, she spoke of the "pantheism of art," indicating that she values all musical modes of being. But the decision to head out and change the world of popular music, particularly country, was refined by her manager, Larry Wanagas. When Wanagas met lang, lang said she wanted to be a jazz singer. Wanagas encouraged her instead to become established as a musician in some other genre before turning to jazz, as he explained to Stern: "I said if you want to be a jazz singer the first thing to do is to build yourself a little platform so that once you have some notoriety and success, you have a lot easier time with it. If we start pushing you as a jazz singer at twenty years old, we're all going to starve."

A Rocker in the Country

In choosing country, lang moved to a form of music that is indigenous to the area in which she grew up — it is familiar. Whether this has made for a more "honest" body of recordings is open to question, because one genre of music is not necessarily any more "honest" than another. Rock, for example, is no more artificial or contrived than country. In both, a musician adopts an artistic stance and tries to convey certain emotional states within the strictures of a song. Of course, rock's concerns tend to be urban ones while those of country are rural. But the creative process common to both is the use of musical and poetic symbols to provide a heightened human experience; in that sense, both are artificial. Similarly, their subject matter is often the same. For both, the highway is a symbol of escape or exile. For both, unrequited love (or perhaps in rock, that of insatiable love) is the central theme.

That lang consciously chose country music as her genre is remarkable. The path to success — or at least vigorous activity — for virtually all popular musicians is a meandering one, with chance encounters. Furthermore, a popular musician usually has a genre that he or she has either found success in or has shown a particular aptitude for. To step onto the sunny road to artistic success simply because one decides it is the right thing to do is surely a sign of lang's determination and self-confidence. Of course, with a view of her music as a means of performance, lang could conceivably decide, without much warning, to follow a musical direction completely different from the one she is now taking. If she did change musical direction, she would have many options: rock, jazz or even the country swing she began with. One thing is certain: it would be very difficult to maintain a single direction indefinitely. The Romaniac Brothers, an "ethno-fusion" band, have learned this lesson to their detriment. Their music falls into two categories: "rockifications" of eastern European chord progressions and rhythms, and the reverse, "ethnicization" of rock and pop standards. (Many of their songs, in fact, have the feel of lang's "Watch Your Step Polka," from *Angel with a Lariat*.) In spite of national television and radio appearances, the band could not secure a recording contract. It was seen as a "novelty" act, a fad.

Lang is the first popular musician to make country music appeal to the general audience usually devoted to rock musicians. *A Truly Western Experience, Angel with a Lariat* and *Absolute Torch and Twang* all feature lang's blend of country songs — some written by others, some by lang — and pop songs. Some songs, of course, include both influences. Lang has shown that you can dance to country music in something other than the square-dance mode.

The influence of country music has always been a part of rock, but as a distinct idiom it has always been considered by rock audiences to be the antithesis of rock. Still, the first dramatic sign of k.d. lang's growing fame was a two-thirds page feature in the "Music News" section of a rock journal, not a country and western publication. The June 20, 1985, edition of *Rolling Stone* featured "Canadian Cowpunk," an item that reported on lang's appearance at New York's Bottom Line: "She turned in a kinetic performance, do-si-do-ing primly around the stage at one moment and bellowing into the mike with the rage of Johnny Rotten the next." The next time she gained international headlines was her release in 1987 of a duet with Roy Orbison, singing Orbison's standard, "Crying." The song was the basis for a video that received a considerable amount of television air-play.

Lang's success with rock audiences must be attributed at least in part to the fact that rock, in order to renew itself — as it has done for three decades — must occasionally return to its roots. Rock's lyrical and musical references are usually from within rock itself. The motive of sexual adolescence, for example, is not treated extensively in any other musical genre. Similarly, the musical structures of rock are relatively simple and must be kept so, if the music is to remain accessible to its audience. Rock begins to suffer from artistic entropy if it does not find some source of energy outside itself. By turning to its roots of blues and country, rock is able to borrow — and exchange, of course, for the transaction is not unidirectional — musical and lyrical elements. In Canada, country roots, unlike those of blues, are as indigenous as they are in the US.

The central archetype of country music — the cowboy, or the country singer himself — has much in common with the central archetype of rock, the rock singer himself. Both figures have turned their backs on society's conventions. Both travel alone. Both use the guitar as a symbol of the solitary romantic predicament. That is why performers as diverse as Leonard Cohen and Ian Tyson have cultivated the image of the cowboy and found artistic inspiration in its myths. Cohen, for example, grew up listening to country music and, early in his career, even lived on a ranch near Nashville. For his part, Tyson lives on a ranch in southern Alberta — bought with the royalties he earned when Neil Young covered "Four Strong Winds" on *Comes a Time* — where he raises cutting horses.

In the popular music of the 1980s, Elvis Costello was the first rocker to revive interest in country music. When asked to explain the attraction of the music for him, he has said, "Perhaps I am fascinated by tainted love." Of course, Neil Young has played country music off and on since the beginning of his career. But whereas Young adopts country as a style of composition, without trying to change it, lang, like Costello, allows it to function only as an influence. While Young uses country as an *alternative* to rock, both Costello and lang use it as a means of enlivening and re-creating rock.

It is one thing for a rocker such as Elvis Costello to incorporate country music into his compositions; it is another for lang. She is the first woman to find and embrace the libidinous drive of country music. First impressions of her act, as indicated in the "Canadian Cowpunk" item from *Rolling Stone*, often conjure up the names of male rockers. When combined with her relatively low voice and her appearance — her short hair and the farmhand outfit on the cover of *Absolute Torch and Twang* — it makes for an androgynous image. Where her female colleagues favour long hair (or, in some cases, "big" hair) and dress in provocative outfits, lang opts to avoid the stereotypical appearance of the country "torch" look. Furthermore, among female country singers, only lang includes the up-tempo, rock-influenced songs of country music in her repertoire. On a personal level, however, lang's aspirations to rock music are not matched by the hard-driving lifestyle that often appeals to rock's performers. She is a vegetarian and doesn't smoke or drink. In 1985, she told *Canadian Composer* magazine that she never touched "recreational drugs."

Challenging the Boundaries of Country

Despite lang's role as an iconoclast, many of the songs she has recorded were, in fact, written by other musicians. That she does not sing exclusively original material means she is often *interpreting*, a role that is relatively rare in country music. (Typically, country singers sing their own songs. It is the most effective way to maintain the sincerity and honesty that, for much of the audience of country music, are among the most appealing attributes of the art form.) The significance of this is that lang has, thus far in her career, cast herself in the position of someone who is interacting with the tradition of country music, rather than absorbing or assimilating it. She has chosen the aspects of country music that she finds attractive or compelling: the energy of the square dance, the directness of the cowboy's narrative stance and the drama (and humour) of western outfits. Still, aside from *Shadowland*, which features no compositions by lang, the proportion of lang compositions (or joint compositions including lang) has increased from one-third (on her first album) to one-half (on *Angel with a Lariat*) to three-quarters (on *Absolute Torch and Twang*). Gradually, she is turning to an effort to enlarge country music's borders and away from an examination of country music's influence on her.

Lang's recordings illustrate her determination to continue to change country music. The first couple of albums were modest efforts. (*A Truly Western Experience*, for example, cost only $5,000 to produce and record.) Still, both established Lang's reputation as a new and aggressive voice in country and popular music. In particular, *Angel with a Lariat* turned out to be lang's most turbo-charged album — it is the one that combines, most powerfully, rock riffs with the square-dance beat. *Shadowland*, on the other hand, was, even for lang, a departure. Released on the Sire label (of Talking Heads and Madonna fame), the album has none of the pop or cowpunk sounds that appear on all her other albums. The album helped lang sweep the Canadian Country Music Awards in 1989. (Lang is no stranger to awards. Also in 1989, lang won three honours at the Canadian Country Music Awards: best entertainer, best album [for *Shadowland*], and best female vocalist. She has won two Grammys: one in 1989 for her duet with Roy Orbison ["Crying"] and one in 1990 for best female country vocalist. Also in 1990, she won the Juno for best female country vocalist.)

The songs on *Shadowland* evoke the sound of the late Patsy Cline. Early in her career as a singer-songwriter, lang happily stated that she was the reincarnation of Patsy Cline, who, in 1963, died in a plane crash while only in her early thirties. As lang's media attention has increased, however, lang has found that personal views such as the one about reincarnation make her vulnerable to ridicule and misunderstanding. As a result, she doesn't talk about that aspect of her beliefs anymore. She told *Billboard*, "At one point I felt very strongly about letting people know how I felt about (personal beliefs), but North Americans aren't really that open-minded when it comes to things like reincarnation." At least one incident in lang's life is, if nothing else, coincidental. As described in a *Billboard* article, after one of her concerts in Nashville in 1987, lang left the building and, letting a balloon float up into the sky, said, "Here, Patsy." After watching the balloon float away, she turned around to find Charlie Dick, Cline's widower. The two met for the first time.

One of the most refreshing aspects of *Shadowland* is its aural consistency. Here, lang's skills as a performance artist are focused on creating a highly unified style. Because that style is the Nashville sound of the 1940s and 1950s, she sings only songs by the writers of that period. This is the only album that does not feature any original compositions. The string arrangements, the use of slide guitar, and the backup vocals by the Jordanaires all contribute to a unified style, a quality that most solo artists are able to achieve only after the release of many albums. There is no "Hooked on Junk" here. Having Owen Bradley produce the album was an obvious influence in this regard.

But lang's voice is the controlling influence on *Shadowland*, expressing various shades of emotion while maintaining a consistent mood. It is the most impressive accomplishment on the album. Like the glasses, lang's voice has resulted in much journalistic commentary and interest. It would be unique in any musical genre. She is an alto, so her voice is stronger and lower than that of most female country singers. Some listeners find it masculine. For every song she sings, it provides the qualities of energy and power. At times, it becomes a wail, evoking the starkness that is absent from so much other country music. In terms of her technique, she uses whatever she can to create the dramatic moment. For example, she frequently uses glissando (sliding up to and down from notes). She also uses many other "tricks" of singing, such as preceding the vibrato portion of a note with non-vibrato. She avoids the "grace notes" (the technique of briefly preceding a tone with another tone, usually a step or half step below) that her colleagues tend to favour. A neat trick that she uses often to good effect is that of allowing the note to soar upward in pitch and waver near the top of her range. On some songs, lang's voice sounds — if not androgynous — then a bit like an enthusiastic boy whose voice has not yet changed.

Shadowland is, in short, lang's best "performance" as a performance artist. Through the use of whatever means she can conjure (including the listener's own memory of some of these well-known songs), lang attempts to initiate the synergy of effects that is the mark of the best performance art.

On Her Own: Making "Honest" Music Work

That Absolute Torch and Twang, the next release, has so many personal touches is, in part, a statement against the forces that tended to hem in lang a bit on the other albums. After all, her second and third albums were recorded in London, England, and all of her early albums were produced by relative outsiders to lang's music. This one was recorded in Canada, with lang as a co-producer. One gets the sense that Absolute Torch and Twang is the first one of lang's albums on which she did not get a lot of help from pop's "geniuses"; she is on her own now. In addition to references to the wind of the prairies, there are repeated personal references. This is a more introspective album than any of the others.

After taking a hiatus during the recording of Shadowland, lang's band the Reclines returned for the recording of Absolute Torch and Twang. One band member, Ben Mink (who lang met at Expo 85 in Japan), co-produced and co-wrote Absolute Torch and Twang; he also plays violin, guitar and mandolin on the album. He is formerly of Silver Tractors fame. Mink's contribution — and you can hear his influence, if you listen carefully to other albums he has worked on, including Murray

McLauchlan's *Boulevard* — is in the stark, open sound of songs such as "Luck in My Eyes" and "Nowhere to Stand."

Both lang and Mink state that their goal is to make music that is "honest" and "pure." They say that Nashville has recently begun to pay too much attention to helping songs "cross over" into the pop market and not enough attention to encouraging a distinctive country style. Mink explained it this way in *Canadian Musician*: "At one point Nashville had a serious problem about being regarded as hicks. Then they got glitzy. A couple of artists had crossover country hits and then everybody tried it. In doing that they diluted what was pure and honest about (country music) and it became a mish-mash.... I think it's the damage people like Kenny Rogers have done. Even though *he's* great, the people who try to imitate him are way off the mark." While working to change country and popular music, lang uses individuality and sincerity as the criteria by which she judges the quality of her music. It is interesting to recall that one of her Juno "wedding vows" was that she would always sing "for the right reasons."

Absolute Torch and Twang begins with "Luck in the My Eyes," a song that compares the weather of the prairies with the psychic terrain — it is really the first time that lang has dealt directly with the prairies as a geographical entity. There's none of the rock influence that was in evidence on *Angel with a Lariat*. Still, the album has a high proportion of bopping. "Big Big Love," written by Wynn Stewart, is the most driving example of this.

Songs on the album dealing with the motives of hidden sorrow and honesty are "It's Me" and "Nowhere to Stand." "It's Me" is about the familiar theme of the dichotomy between appearance and reality in popular music: the singer assures her lover that her television image is not creeping into her private life. The final song on the album, "Nowhere to Stand," is an intimate reflection on the irony of "family values." The song speaks of a woman, who is now also a mother, and her childhood hurts. Its reference to a small town is not incidental, because life in a small Canadian town calls for adherence to accepted patterns of behaviour and appearance. For those growing up there, the only alternatives are conformity or exodus.

Absolute Torch and Twang is in many ways a culmination of lang's artistic convictions and accomplishments. I have never seen a more guileless album cover released by a prairie musician. The title of the album does not actually appear on either the front or back covers except in small print on the edge (the side you see if you stack an LP in an upright position). As a result, there is nothing to distract the viewer from the figure (lang herself) and the ground (the prairie). If it is possible for an artistic creation to convey honesty, then this cover does. Lang is dressed for chores. It's the rural "layered" look: black t-shirt under an authentically faded denim jacket under, in turn, a well-worn suede waistcoat. She is standing in a field of wheat that has been threshed but not baled. In her hands are a pair of old leather gloves and a grey stetson. She wears little or no make-up. She is looking away. In the upper-right section of the photograph is an abandoned wooden granary.

What is truly striking about the album cover is not some aspect of her figure or anatomy — as in the case of the covers for many of her female colleagues in country music — but the colours of sky and field. The sky is indigo, the colour of a prairie autumn sky and, of course, denim. The field is the colour of grain that is just past the flush of ripening. Lang's "blue," then, is an entirely different shade from Joni Mitchell's "blue" (as seen on her album of that name), although both women began their lives viewing the same sky. Mitchell's is Prussian blue — a painter's hue — that evokes, not the blues of the south, but the city's phosphorescence. It is the midnight blue that provides a backdrop for the silver jewellery in "Carey." Lang's blue is the promise of the open sky, the blue-black reflected in the tiny, reedy lakes of Alberta and Saskatchewan. Similarly, the coyote lang sings to in "Full Moon Full of Love" is a wilder animal than the one Mitchell addresses in *Hejira*.

Referring to *Absolute Torch and Twang*, lang told *Canadian Living*, "This [album] is probably the first time I have ever truly revealed that many aspects of me: the writing, the production, being absolutely myself on the cover. I feel a little more at ease gaining a certain level of acceptance. It relaxes me." In the same interview, she said, "I like grain elevators." John Rockwell, an American music critic, said in his book *All American Music* that "Deeper, more personal values, the kind best cultivated in geographic or spiritual isolation, can be mislaid in the pursuit of instantaneous success." Perhaps lang senses the need to establish her identity now, rather than waiting until sustained commercial success has been assured. She has yet to attain the kind of success that would intrude on her privacy and her ability to reflect.

Absolute Torch and Twang is thus evidence of both accomplishment and promise. The album is full of subtle marvels. For example, the fretless bass playing usually associated with jazz, heard on "Trail of Broken Hearts" creates the forlorn feeling suggested by the song's lyrics. It is this kind of touch that will allow lang to expand her musical scope on future albums to include whatever influences she wants.

Lang's appeal, finally, must be that she has embraced a musical idiom and changed the assumptions of its audience. Lang has brought a new perspective to country, of country as simply one influence among many that may be used by a popular singer-songwriter to pursue those elusive musical and lyrical qualities of immediacy and integrity. While it is difficult to define these qualities, there is no doubt when a musician has them. And lang has them. Her compositional skills are still developing, but her collaborations with Ben Mink show much promise. Whether or not lang continues to mine the vein of country music, whatever she does in music, she will be a transforming presence — someone whose desire to express her artistic convictions is so strong that it foils the commercial forces of popular music.

k.d. lang — The Best

Song: "Didn't I"

Album: *Absolute Torch and Twang*

Article for further reading: "Voice from the West: The k.d. lang Success Story Involves Much More Than Luck," *Canadian Composer*, December 1985, pp. 4-10+.

Discography

A Truly Western Experience (1984)
Angel With a Lariat (1987)
Shadowland: The Owen Bradley Sessions (1988)
Absolute Torch and Twang (1989)

References

General References
Sources listed below are books that I refer to or quote from at various points throughout the text.
Audley, Paul. *Canada's Cultural Industries: Broadcasting, Publishing, Records and Film.* Toronto: James Lorimer & Co./Canadian Institute for Economic Policy, 1983.
Bookbinder, David. *What Folk Music Is All About.* New York: Julian Messner, 1979.
Eisen, Jonathan, ed. *The Age of Rock: Sounds of the American Cultural Revolution.* Toronto: Random House of Canada Ltd., 1969.
Ellmann, Richard, and Robert O'Clair, eds. *The Norton Anthology of Modern Poetry.* New York: W.W. Norton & Company, Inc., 1973.
Manoff, Tom. *Music: A Living Language.* New York: W.W. Norton & Company, 1982.
Marcus, Greil. *Mystery Train: Images of America in Rock 'n' Roll Music.* New York: E.P. Dutton & Co., Inc., 1975.
Melhuish, Martin. *Heart of Gold: 30 Years of Canadian Pop Music.* Toronto: CBC Enterprises, 1983.
Miller, Jim, ed. *The Rolling Stone Illustrated History of Rock & Roll.* Revised and Updated. Toronto: Random House, 1980.
Pattison, Robert. *The Triumph of Vulgarity: Rock Music in the Mirror of Romanticism.* New York: Oxford University Press, 1987.
Rockwell, John. *All American Music: Composition in the Late Twentieth Century.* New York: Alfred A. Knopf, Inc., 1983.
Yorke, Ritchie. *Axes, Chops and Hot Licks: The Canadian Rock Music Scene.* Edmonton: M.G. Hurtig Ltd., Publishers, 1971.

Other Sources — Listed by Chapter
In addition to the books listed in the general reference list, I used information for each chapter from books and from articles in various magazines, newspapers and academic journals. The following is a list of the most important of these, including those from which I have quoted significantly.

Lightfoot
Beyer, Susan. "Lightfoot Leaves Fans Clamoring for More." *Ottawa Citizen*, Nov. 23, 1988.
Collins, Maynard. *Lightfoot: If You Could Read His Mind.* Toronto: Deneau, 1988.
Coppage, Noel. "Gordon Lightfoot." *Stereo Review* 34 (April 1975), p. 54.
_____. "Gordon Lightfoot's *Summertime Dream*: Running Over with Poetry." *Stereo Review* 37 (October 1976), p. 87.
_____. "In the Matter of Gordon Lightfoot." *Stereo Review* 33 (August 1974), p. 88.
"Gordon Lightfoot: A Special Section." *Billboard* 87 (Apr. 5, 1975), p. GL 1.
Hopkins, Tom. "Gordon's Song." *Maclean's*, May 1, 1978, p. 30.
Howard, John Tasker. *Stephen Foster: America's Troubadour.* New York: Thomas Y. Crowell, 1935.
McLauchlan, Murray. "Gordon Lightfoot." *Canadian Composer* n. 214 (October 1986), p. 4.
"New Acts." *Variety* 239 (July 7, 1965), p. 50.
"Record Review: *Endless Wire*." *High Fidelity/Musical America* 28 (April 1978), p. 138.
Ross, Penelope. "Canada's Most Successful Singer-Songwriter Talks About His Music." *Canadian Composer* n. 99 (March 1975), p. 4.

Cohen
Batten, Jack. "Leonard Cohen: The Poet as Hero." *Saturday Night*, June 1969, p. 23.
Bonzai, Mr. "Leonard Cohen: Haute Dog." *Mix*, March 1989, p. 66.
Bowering, George. "Inside Leonard Cohen." *Canadian Literature* 33 (Summer 1967), p. 71.
"Canadian Poet Len Cohen Turning Folksinger-Cleffer." *Variety* 245 (Feb. 15, 1967), p. 43.
Chaffin, Tom. "Conversations from a Room." *Canadian Forum*, August/September 1983, p. 7.

Collie, Ashley. "Leonard Cohen: Old Skin for the New Ceremony." *Canadian Musician* 7, n. 4, 1985, p. 44.

Cott, Jonathan. "Cohen Conquers Carnegie." *Rolling Stone* n. 450 (June 20, 1985), p. 20.

DiMartino, Dave. "Cohen Has New Disk, Same Ol' Sense of Humor." *Billboard* 100 (May 21, 1988), p. 31.

Djwa, Sandra. "Leonard Cohen: Black Romantic." *Canadian Literature* 34 (Autumn 1967), p. 32.

Holden, Stephen. "A Haunting by Spector." *Rolling Stone* n. 257 (Jan. 26, 1978), p. 17.

Kirk, Kris. "Poetry Commotion." *Melody Maker* 64 (June 18, 1988), p. 43.

LeBlanc, Larry. "Cohen's Life Counts First; Poetry Is Reflection." *Music Scene* n. 258 (March-April 1971), p. 4.

Mortifoglio, Richard. "Leonard Cohen Dies the Small Death." *Village Voice* 23 (Jan. 2, 1978), p. 55

Ondaatje, Michael. *Leonard Cohen.* Toronto: McClelland and Stewart, 1970.

Pacey, Desmond. "The Phenomenon of Leonard Cohen." *Canadian Literature* 34 (Autumn 1967), p. 5.

Rowland, Mark. "Leonard Cohen's Nervous Breakthrough." *Musician* n. 117 (July 1988), p. 94.

Scobie, Stephen. *Leonard Cohen.* Vancouver: Douglas & McIntyre, 1978.

____. "Magic, Not Magicians." *Canadian Literature* 45 (Summer 1970), p. 56.

Wayne, Joyce. "Interview with Leonard Cohen." *Quill & Quire*, May 1984, p. 4.

Young

Cocks, Jay. "Dylan and Young on the Road." *Time*, Nov. 6, 1978, p. 89.

Crowe, Cameron. "Neil Young: The Last American Hero." *Rolling Stone* n. 284 (Feb. 8, 1979), p. 41.

____. "Neil Young: The *Rolling Stone* Interview." *Rolling Stone* n. 193 (Aug. 14, 1975), p. 36.

Flanagan, Bill. "The Real Neil Young Stands Up." *Musician* n. 85 (November 1985), p. 32.

Hampton, Howard. "Let It Blurt." *Village Voice* 32 (Sept. 8, 1987), p. 72.

Hull, R.A. "Too Young to Rust, Too Old to Die." *Creem* 12 (February 1981), p. 32.

"New Acts." *Variety* 254 (Feb. 19, 1969), p. 68.

"Pop! The Glory Years." *Melody Maker* 63 (Oct. 17, 1987), p. 8.

Rogan, Johnny. *Neil Young: The Definitive Story of His Musical Career.* London: Proteus, 1982.

Rowland, Mark. "Cruise Control: Neil Young's Lonesome Drive." *Musician* n. 116 (June 1988), p. 62.

Young, Scott. *Neil and Me.* Toronto: McClelland and Stewart, 1984.

Mitchell

Coppage, Noel. "Innocence on a Spree." *Stereo Review* 36 (April 1976), p. 4.

Crowe, Cameron. "Joni Mitchell: The *Rolling Stone* Interview." *Rolling Stone* n. 296 (July 26, 1979), p. 46.

Feldman, Jim. "Review: *Wild Things Run Fast.*" *Creem* 14 (February 1983), p. 53.

Flanagan, Bill. "Joni Mitchell Loses Her Cool." *Musician* n. 86 (December 1985), p. 64.

____. "Secret Places." *Musician* n. 115 (May 1988), p. 64.

Heckman, Don. "Joni Mitchell: She Soars, She Orbits, She Never Lands." *High Fidelity/Musical America* 28 (March 1978), p. 136

Holden, Stephen. "Joni Mitchell's Live Album Is a Surprise and a Triumph." *Rolling Stone* n. 330 (Nov. 13, 1980), p. 57.

____. "A 'Summer' Garden of Verse." *Rolling Stone* n. 204 (Jan. 15, 1976), p. 50.

"New Acts." *Variety* 244 (Sept. 21, 1966), p. 61.

Pond, Steve. "Wild Things Run Fast." *Rolling Stone* n. 383 (Nov. 25, 1982), p. 70.

Swartley, Ariel. "Mitchell: The Siren and the Symbolist." Rolling Stone, n. 232 (Feb. 10, 1977), p. 99.

Cockburn

Emerson, Ken. "Mystic from the North." *Rolling Stone* n. 278 (Nov. 16, 1978), p. 32.

Gilday, Katherine. "Cockburn's Act Polished, Simple." *Globe and Mail*, Oct. 30, 1978, p. 16.

Hoffman, Jan. "Bruce Cockburn's Nice Distinction." *Village Voice* 23 (May 8, 1978), p. 51.
Holden, Stephen. "Bruce Cockburn's Quiet Optimism." *High Fidelity/Musical America* 31 (January 1981), p. 83.
Kostash, Myrna. "The Pure, Uncluttered Spaces of Bruce Cockburn." *Saturday Night*, June 1972, p. 21.
Lacy, Liam. "Cockburn's Glory More Than a Rumor." *Globe and Mail*, Aug. 12, 1982, p. 17.
Lake, Steve. "Casting Light in the Falling Dark." *Melody Maker* 56 (Mar. 21, 1981), p. 27.
McKendrick, Coral. "Cockburn All-Canadian by Choice." Winnipeg Free Press, July 13, 1978, p. 29.
"New Acts." Variety 253 (Nov. 20, 1968), p. 84.
Radz, Matt. "Interview." *Montreal Star*, Mar. 24, 1979, p. D5.
Testa, Bart. "Royal Canadians." *Crawdaddy* n. 61 (June 1976), p. 69.

McLauchlan
"Comeback Year for McLauchlan." *Performing Arts Canada* no. 4 (1978), p. 15.
Erlich, Nancy. "Concert Review (Lori Lieberman, Murray McLauchlan)." *Billboard* 86 (May 18, 1974), p. 22.
Flohil, Richard. "Murray McLauchlan: Back on the Street." *Canadian Composer* n. 61 (June 1971), p. 4.
Holden, Stephen. "Murray McLauchlan: True Blue-Collar Grit." *Rolling Stone* n. 258 (Feb. 9, 1978), p. 17.
Kostash, Myrna. "Macho Murray and Me." *Saturday Night*, April 1977, p. 20.
Lacey, Liam. "Edmonton Folk Festival in Tune with Its Audience." *Globe and Mail*, Aug. 10, 1987, p. C9.
"New Acts." *Variety* 244 (Oct. 19, 1966), p. 52.
"Taking Canadian Music to the World." *Canadian Composer* n. 126 (December 1977), p. 18.
Testa, Bart. "Royal Canadians." *Crawdaddy* n. 61 (June 1976), p. 69.

Siberry
Bessman, Jim. "Reprise's Siberry Peddles Clip at Shows." *Billboard* 100 (May 28, 1988), p. 51.
Druckman, Howard. "Jane Siberry: Extending the Boundaries of Pop Music." *Canadian Musician* 10, n. 1, 1988, p. 10.
Eichenwald, Wes. "Saturday Review Talks to Jane Siberry." *Saturday Review* 12 (January/February 1986), p. 92.
Kelley, Linda. "Jane Siberry's Musical Dance in and out of Time." *Canadian Composer* n. 204 (October 1985), p. 4.
Kirk, Kris. "Mystery Tour." *Melody Maker* 64 (Aug. 6, 1988), p. 18.
_____. "Pixie on Acid?" *Melody Maker* 63 (July 11, 1987), p. 13.
Roberts, Chris. "Walking on Water." *Melody Maker* 64 (June 11, 1988), p. 37.
Shewey, Don. "Record Review: *No Borders Here*." *Rolling Stone* n. 451 (July 4, 1985), p. 53.
Straessle, Carla. "Jane Siberry." *Canadian Musician* 7, no. 1, 1985, p. 30.
Sutherland, Steve. "Cry Woolf." *Melody Maker* 64 (Apr. 30, 1988), p. 34.
Switzer, John. "Stage and Studio: Defining the Difference." *Canadian Musician* 10, no. 4, 1988, p. 24.
Wilde, Jonh. "Flowing Muses." *Melody Maker* 64 (Aug. 6, 1988), p. 8.

Lang
"Canadian Cowpunk." *Rolling Stone* n. 450 (June 20, 1985), p. 76.
"Concert Review (Dwight Yoakum, Buck Owens, k.d. lang)." *Variety* 332 (Aug. 10, 1988), p. 50.
Flohil, Richard. "Voice from the West." *Canadian Composer* n. 206 (December 1985), p. 4.
Myers, Caren. "Concert Review (Lyle Lovett, k.d. lang)." *Melody Maker* 64 (June 25, 1988), p. 21.
Stanley, Shelagh. "Country Music Sings a New Tune." *Canadian Living*, November 1989, p. 39.
Stern, Perry. "k.d. lang: Sustaining the Edge." *Canadian Musician* 9, no. 2, 1987, p. 28.
Wood, Gerry. "Canada's k.d. lang Gains Acceptance." *Billboard* 100 (Sept. 26, 1987), p. 44.